Blitzing Vauxhall

A Dogsbody's War Diary

Owen Hardisty

The
Book
Castle

Dedicated to the memory of Arnold (Arthur) Fulcher,
"gentleman's gentleman", Norfolk rebel and a friend of the underdog.

Dedication to Owen

December 23rd 1925–May 15th 2005

This book will stand as a tribute to Owen and all those who helped
make it possible.

Owen's exceptional general knowledge, humour and wit were only matched
by his stature at six foot five inches. He was truly a gentle giant
and a loyal friend.

Certain in his own beliefs, he loved to argue and debate on any subject and
had great admiration for craftsmanship, whether of hand or brain.

Owen knew without any doubt that the English countryside was
incomparable at every season and spent many hours painting it in
watercolour, to the sound of varied music that portrayed his catholic tastes.

His wife, family and friends will cherish this book.

First published September 2005
by The Book Castle, 12 Church Street, Dunstable, Bedfordshire LU5 4RU

© Owen Hardisty, 2005

The right of Owen Hardisty to be identified as the Author of this work has been asserted
by him in accordance with the Copyright, Designs and Patents Act, 1988

ISBN 1 903747 62 7

Designed and typeset by Caroline and Roger Hillier, The Old Chapel Graphic Design

Printed in Great Britain by Antony Rowe Ltd., Chippenham, Wiltshire

Front cover picture: The morning after – the scene in K block

Contents

Acknowledgements iv

Preface v

About the Author vi

Introduction vii

CHAPTER ONE Bad omens at Yarmouth 1
August–December 1939

CHAPTER TWO A long bitter winter 15
January–April 1940

CHAPTER THREE Vauxhall – first impressions 23
April–June 1940

CHAPTER FOUR Dunkirk – digging in 49
June–July 1940

CHAPTER FIVE The onslaught begins 57
July–September 1940

CHAPTER SIX Alarms by night and day 83
September–November 1940

CHAPTER SEVEN Smoke screen, bombs and exhaustion 99
November–December 1940

CHAPTER EIGHT Our meagre Christmas 109
December 1940

CHAPTER NINE New Year – new hope 123
January–December 1941

EPILOGUE 143

ACKNOWLEDGEMENTS

My thanks to the following for their much appreciated help in producing "BLITZING VAUXHALL"

Luton News Editor John Buckledee for permission to publish historic photographs from the Luton News collection held by Luton Museum Service.
Luton Museum Service photographic officer, Chris Grabham, for his help in locating and reproducing historic photographs.
Luton Museum Service and Vauxhall Heritage Centre for allowing access to their archives.
Vauxhall Heritage Centre archivist/photographer, Dennis Sherer, for his patience and invaluable help in digging out rare gems from his vast collection.
My fellow U3A member, Colin Cook, for posing with WW2 fire watcher's equipment at his "Museum in the Garden".
Author Robert Cook for his advice and encouragement.
My old Vauxhall colleague, ex apprentice and engineer, Chris Rigby, for jolting my memory.
Luton U3A Local history group co-ordinator, Diane Cullen, for her many hours of work and her expertise in transcribing my manuscript.

Grateful thanks are due to the following for the photographs reproduced in this book:
Vauxhall Motors Heritage Centre archives
Luton News for photographs held by Luton Museum Service
Luton News for advertisements from Luton Library collection
Other line illustrations and photographs are by the author

Bibliography
Vauxhall A Century in Motion. 1903–2003. David Burgess Wise.
Luton at War. Luton News.
An Account of our Stewardship. W. J. Seymour.

PREFACE

Owen Hardisty has written a fascinating and compelling account of his very young days working at Vauxhall in Luton during the blitz of World War II. Taken from his daily diary, written since his schooldays, it really is a wonderful historical record as well as a graphic personal account of life, most of it spent working in the Luton plant producing military vehicles and thus being a prime target for Nazi bombers. It is difficult to imagine what it must have been like on the ground, waiting for bombs to fall with the prospect of a violent death at any moment, but Owen's brilliant description brings that time alive. I could not put down the pre-publication script which I read from beginning to end.

While a good few years younger than Owen (I was born in 1941), I do remember the tail end of the war and sitting in an Anderson Shelter in the next door neighbour's garden in South London at the age of 2 while watching London burning in the distance. I remember my mother taking myself and my brother Tim (now a retired teacher living in Luton) to stay with my grandparents in Leicester shortly before a V-1 flying bomb landed in our South London back garden and blew up the house while my father was at work. I was too young to appreciate that these were fearful events but Owen Hardisty's fine writing brings the terror of the blitz to life again and reminds us that dreadful things happen in war.

But Owen's book is also about Luton and the happier moments in a young man's life, enjoying the town and the countryside around, and friendship and family. Thousands of older Lutonians will recall the town as it was in those days, and indeed I am familiar with much of what Owen describes from my own 36 years in Luton. His eye for detail in his account of the ordinary events of a young life as well as the extraordinary events of war is always interesting.

I have known the Hardisty family since shortly after I came to Luton. I remember that Owen's late brother, Ivor, helped me get elected to Luton Council for the old Stopsley Ward in 1972, more than half way back in time to the events Owen describes in his book.

Owen Hardisty's book is alive and vivid and I know it will be read by thousands in Luton with the greatest enjoyment, an account of desperate days which Britain and Luton survived. Yes, we survived the war, but at that time there was a very real fear that Britain would be overrun by the Nazis. Owen brilliantly evokes those times and he must be congratulated on a remarkable book.

Kelvin Hopkins MP, Luton North

ABOUT THE AUTHOR

Owen Hardisty was born in Letchworth Garden City in 1925 and educated at the local school, which he left in April 1940 aged 14 to join Vauxhall as an office boy at a salary of fourteen shillings and sixpence (72p) a week.

In 1942 he gained an apprenticeship in Vauxhall's Trade School and trained for a career in Quality Control, meantime attending evening and day release classes at Luton Technical College.

In the middle years of the war, aged seventeen, he, like many apprentices, enrolled in Vauxhall's Home Guard Company: he later served with the RAF in Egypt and Palestine and on demobilization returned to Vauxhall Motors as an engine test bed inspector.

In 1952 he married Maureen, a London evacuee whose family had settled in Luton, and during the 1950s they had two daughters and a son.

Owen was employed at all three Vauxhall plants, being seconded to Merseyside in 1963, returning to Luton, and finally joining the GM Commercial office as a Supplier Quality Assurance engineer responsible for the conformity to GM Quality Standards of Vauxhall's suppliers in the UK and Europe.

In 1983 GM abandoned commercial vehicle production in Europe and he chose early retirement after 43 years with Vauxhall.

During the past ten years Owen was a regular exhibitor at Luton Arts Council and Wardown Museum art exhibitions and an active member of Luton U3A Local History Group two.

INTRODUCTION

Bill Sibley, captain of the 2nd Letchworth company of the Boy's Brigade, sold me my first pocket diary emblazoned with the BB anchor and their motto, "Sure and steadfast", about the time when Neville Chamberlain returned from Munich waving his worthless paper and promising "peace in our time"; and on the first of January 1939 I made my first daily entry, recording my attendance at North Avenue Mission bible class and the weather, "cold with thawing snow".

In the Spring of that year I left the Boy's Brigade, having outgrown rhythmic Indian club swinging and fed up with bible class and marching behind our bugle and drum band, but my habit of recording daily events continued without pause to the present time; my fondly preserved diaries a chronicle of the ordinary and extraordinary happenings in my life during the past sixty four years. All the entries without exception are laconic single sentences which could not, and were not intended to, convey the reality of past events; it is left to memory to provide the details and evoke the atmosphere of those days, the fear and tragedy, the discomforts, the boredom and humour of the Blitz, the towering exhilaration of VE day, the grief felt on the death of parents, siblings and friends, the joy of our wedding day and the birth of children and grandchildren, but every brief entry is charged with the power to release a flood of recollection and clothe the bare bones of my journal with substance.

I kept my diary throughout the war and subsequent service with the RAF in Egypt and Palestine, through my 43 years with Vauxhall and twenty years of retirement; and it was whilst browsing through the diaries that the idea of a book, compiled from these handwritten notes and the still vivid springs of memory, germinated; an account of the quiet, almost stealthy slide into war and the silly illusions of 1939, the disillusions, anxieties and bitter recriminations of the spring, summer and autumn of 1940 when the harsh reality of the Dunkirk debacle and the ensuing Blitzkrieg faced us all with a rude awakening to our peril and the impact of these events on a fourteen year old school leaver plunging into the adult world of work at a time when all hell broke loose on the European Continent and Winston Churchill was swept to power.

During the preceding decade, the giant American General Motors Corporation invested many millions in the expansion of Vauxhall's Luton plant and by mid 1940 this huge industrial complex was throbbing night and day to replace the vast amounts of military hardware lost in the Dunkirk disaster and striving to re-equip our forces in time to meet the expected invasion. Preparations by then were well advanced to produce the desperately needed Churchill heavy tank, whilst every week a thousand trucks rolled off the assembly lines and my job as a plant roving errand boy gave me a unique opportunity to observe all this frantic activity and the urgency of the situation, to imprint it unforgettably on my mind and remain so to the present day.

Many of the diary's entries deal with the mundane events of everyday life, and some I have omitted to avoid boring repetition; this accounts for the apparent gaps in the chronology of "A Dogsbody's Diary", but elsewhere I have assiduously avoided exaggeration and have striven to present a factual, accurate and honest account.

A thousand books about the Nazi Blitzrieg have been written and thousands more have celebrated the exploits of our heroic defenders in 1940, but far fewer I believe from the viewpoint of a youngster just becoming aware of World events and at his most impressionable age.

At the time of writing, most of the people mentioned, with the happy exception of my predecessor and mentor Trevor Dean, have long since passed away and the Vauxhall plant I knew in 1940 has mostly vanished; only the shrapnel chipped kerbstones in Kimpton Road give a hint of more violent times to those who know where to look, and the Vauxhall war memorial set amidst the landscaped shrubbery where P Block once stood lists those who died.

On a bitterly cold January morning in 2001, Maureen and I, our daughters and grandson assembled in Kimpton Road with twenty thousand Vauxhall workers, pensioners and their families to march to the town centre in a vain attempt to prevent the closure of Vauxhall after almost a century in Luton. My emotions ran high as we joined the demonstration at the exact spot where I had alighted from the works bus on that April morning in 1940, and where Wally Plumb, the newsvendor whose brother Fred had died fighting the Nazis in Spain, stood with his battered perambulator at W Block gate and whose name is still commemorated in "Plumb's DIY", a shop on the opposite side of the road and now owned by Wally's son Eddie.

As the marching thousands poured down the hill towards the Windmill pub and Vauxhall's Corporate Headquarters, I realised that amongst those marching alongside us with their placards and Union banners was a sizeable contingent of German workers from G.M.'s Adam Opel plants which had once produced munitions for Hitler, and now supporting us in friendship and solidarity – reconciled after more than half a century.

Owen Hardisty 2004

CHAPTER ONE

Bad omens at Yarmouth

August–December 1939

Digging in   The lights go out
Chamberlain's radio announcement
The evacuees arrive   Apprehension grows
Where are the bombers?
Part-time schooling – boredom   The "phoney war"
First blackout Christmas and last "peacetime" feast

Mum, dad, brother Ivor, indeed all of us agreed that our week-long holiday in Great Yarmouth had been a great success; we had seen a man, blazing from head to foot, dive off the pierhead to loud applause, climbed Nelson's column, visited the kipper smokery, gorged ourselves on Italian ice cream and, when the rain fell on Friday, we saw "The Four Feathers" at the Empire Cinema followed by fireworks on Wellington Pier, but even in the midst of all the jollity a dark shadow intruded when a trial ARP blackout was held on Tuesday evening and our pleasures were briefly diverted by radio and newspaper talk of threats, ultimatums, shameful pacts and armies massing on frontiers, and somewhere in our subconscious lurked a suspicion we were afraid to confront – that this could be our last carefree peacetime holiday for some long time.

Our holiday ended on the late Sunday afternoon of the 13th August when we alighted from the Yarmouth coach at Allnutt's Café in Baldock where the Great North Road becomes the High Street and a refreshment stop for all the coaches running from London to Scotland.

The following three weeks were filled with daily visits to the swimming pool on Letchworth's Norton Common, reclining on the terrace in the hot sun, often lingering long into the warm evenings and flirting with the girls under the floodlights or daily roaming the Norton hedgerows with my school friend Russell Rogers and his air rifle, idly shooting at tin cans and sparrows.

Thursday 24th August and my diary notes "the Crisis is on", and the hot weather generated thunderstorms which broke the following afternoon when "Rusty Rogers" and I were caught out as we wandered the Radwell water meadows and trudged home bedraggled and damp.

Saturday 26th August Caught a large toad in our pantry which had somehow managed to sneak in by the back door. In the evening Rusty and I saw "Bulldog Drummond's Secret Police" at the Palace Cinema.

Sunday 27th August The afternoon spent at the swimming pool and in the evening wandered down to the Common to sit on the grass with Mum and Dad and listen to the town band play in the gathering dusk.

Monday 28th August Our radio set, which had failed over a week ago, was returned from the repairer's and working well. The situation in Europe worsens by the day and with war approaching with a terrible inevitability we made plans to dig an air raid trench at the foot of our garden.

Wednesday 30th August Ivor and I started to dig our trench. Swimming in the afternoon, more digging this evening.

Thursday 31st August We continued work on the trench; my diary notes "children to be evacuated tomorrow".

Friday 1st September Shopping in town this morning; the Nazis attacked Poland, and the Poles formally declared war on Germany. We darkened our windows tonight and dimmed our lights by applying "toolmaker's blue" (a dense blue paste), which father brought from work, to the upper part of our light bulbs – not very effective and gave our living room the appearance of a police station by night.

Saturday 2nd September Weather overcast and hot, bought torch batteries and dug deeper into the earth. Tonight was the first official "black out" and the start of a night-time gloom which was to last for almost six years, any breach of which could result in a Court appearance.

Mr Chamberlain had returned from meeting Hitler promising "peace in our time" the day before this cheerful gang of Vauxhall's volunteers paused in their labours for a welcome drink – they obviously doubted the promise and dug in "just in case".

Sunday 3rd September was a typical sunny Sunday morning with an
all-pervading silence, broken only by the whirring of lawnmowers and
the muted sound of our radio; my younger brother Ivor and myself were
now joined by our father delving deep into the earth amongst the
raspberries at the foot of our garden; sweating under a cloudless sky to
throw up a parapet of loose chalk. From time to time we would
straighten up to rest and gaze over the newly harvested fields to the
green trackway of the Icknield Way and Baldock beyond. During the
Munich crisis of the previous year we twelve and thirteen year old
"senior boys" had helped Council workmen dig open trenches in the
school gardens using our father's borrowed spades and raising painful
blisters on our soft hands, so by now, a year later, we considered
ourselves quite experienced little navvies.

It was common knowledge that Letchworth's Kryn and Lahy
steelworks, which had been established in the first World War to
produce artillery shells, was once more turning out munitions, and we
local children perched on the level crossing gates in Works Road,
thrilled to see the unmistakeable shapes of bomb casings stacked in the
railway wagons as they rolled past. We tried to imagine the effect of
high explosive bombs, how big would the craters be? How far would
the blast travel and would we be able to duck in time to avoid the
splinters? But the biggest dread was poison gas; veterans of the conflict
of twenty years ago recalled the ruined lungs and blindness of their
comrades, and no-one doubted the readiness of the Nazis to use it again.

Tom Nimmo, a draughtsman at Kryn and Lahy, was our local air raid
warden and had visited every household in Green Lane, patiently fitting
each member of the family with a gas mask, adjusting the head straps to
ensure a gas-tight fit and demonstrating how to stow the contraption in
a neat square cardboard box which was soon to become the badge of the
wartime civilian and increasingly battered, grubby and dog-eared as the
war dragged on. Tom was also a Communist and doubtless saw his ARP
duties as putting into practice his Party's campaign for deep public

October 1938. Hundreds of volunteers using their own picks and spades dig trenches amongst the allotments on a hillside overlooking the Vauxhall plant. The plume of steam from a London-bound train and the distant West Hill water tower can be seen.

shelters and well organised air raid precautions to meet the coming attack.

At 11 o'clock we paused in our digging to join mother and sister Clarice, huddled round our radio set to hear the funereal voice of Neville Chamberlain announce that we were now at war with Germany and then to return to our task; our heads in a daze of unreality and apprehension. My diary notes: "took refugees into Green Lane", and indeed, during the afternoon groups of bewildered children evacuated from London were seen in the street as kindly lady "billeting officers" sought temporary homes for them.

Monday 4th September We should have returned to school today after the summer holidays, instead we filled sandbags, deepened our trench and blacked out the bedrooms.

Wednesday 6th September The first air raid warning of the war; the sirens howled over the town at 7.30 a m and we stood by our trench in the early morning sunlight, scanning a cloudless sky and straining our ears for signs of approaching bombers. Cinema newsreels had featured the bombing of Madrid and Barcelona and, since Friday, Warsaw was under attack from the same Nazi bomber fleet and everyone expected to suffer a similar fate within hours or days.

As Autumn drew on, however, it soon became apparent that the apocalypse was to be delayed and the delusions of the "phoney war" were eagerly and thankfully embraced by a nervous population. War brought a new urgency to the Government's re-armament programme, and factories which had managed to survive the great depression now had full order books.

I had long been intrigued by father's ornate membership certificate of the Amalgamated Society of Engineers, Machinists, Smiths and Pattern Makers which hung in its oak frame and depicted Stephenson, Boulton and Watt and the heroic figures of two Victorian artisans over whose heads an angel newly descended from heaven held wreaths of laurel – or perhaps halos.

Dad was one of this generation of craftsmen, a toolmaker employed at the Vauxhall works and whose skills were now in great demand; long hours of work were now the norm, and it was rarely before nine in the evening when the Luton bus pulled up under the elms at Norton Post Office and Ivor and I would meet him and, carrying his lunch box, walk home together in the gathering dusk.

Tuesday 19th September School resumed after a two-week delay as our teachers were busy with the reception of the London evacuees;

Norton Road school was host to a school from Tottenham, which meant a double shift system, with the Londoners and their teachers taking over the classrooms in the afternoons whilst we natives were free to wander the streets, fields and woods with our friends, gathering the ripe conkers and gorging ourselves on apples and blackberries. Food rationing had yet to be introduced, so every week when the Co-op mobile shop stopped in Green Lane, mother bought a little extra and our store cupboard soon held a small stock of sugar, preserves and tinned items – not much to withstand a siege but a source of comfort to the mind.

April 1939, and newly completed Vauxhall trenches excavated by volunteer workers eight months previously are inspected by H.M. Inspector General of ARP – Wing Commander Hodsell, Frank Southwell, Vauxhall's ARP Controller, and Managing Director Charles Bartlett. This trench adjoined W Block: Crawley Green Road cemetery and the distant power station cooling towers in St. Mary's Road are visible.

The total blackout demanded by law was difficult to maintain, and Dad and I made improvised shutters of plywood or shed roofing felt nailed to flimsy wooden frames, whilst the haberdashers were overwhelmed with customers clamouring for heavy curtain material and Woolworths and cycle shops soon ran out of torch batteries: the worst effect, however, was the feeling of apprehension and foreboding as we hid and huddled under a blanket of total blackness to await the inevitable bombs.

Boredom soon set in; bored by our daily forays to Norton Common or roaming the banks of the River Ivel and air gun shooting with Russell Rogers in the woods bordering Church meadow, but most of all, bored by the war where nothing seemed to happen and time and conflict were held in suspension.

I bought a Daily Telegraph war map complete with tiny paper flags of Britain, France and Germany where one could plot the positions of the British Expeditionary Force, the impregnable Maginot Line and the Nazis; but month after month those flags moved not one inch.

Apart from rare visits to the Broadway cinema, our only entertainment was the radio and, for the first few weeks, programmes consisted of endless recitals by Sandy McPherson or Reginald Foorte on the cinema organ, interspersed with news bulletins; slowly, however, the BBC reconciled itself to the new conditions and began to offer more uplifting fare with the return of Tommy Handley's "It's that Man Again" on Tuesdays and "Bandwaggon" on Saturday evenings.

Monday, 30th October Our headmaster, Mr Haysman, in a vain attempt to dispel boredom and keep us from mischief, introduced first aid classes for senior pupils which were held in the school's new gymnasium. We spent many hours applying improvised splints to arms and legs, eagerly groping each other's bodies for pressure points to staunch imaginary bleeding and learning the mysteries of the triangular bandage.

A Vauxhall Auxiliary Fire Service crew demonstrate a newly acquired trailer pump to H.M. Inspector General of ARP Wing Commander Hodsell and Company executives on the lorry park on front of Q Block.

Tuesday, 31st October Mr Haysman presented me with a cheque for £2 at this morning's assembly, being first prize in a National essay competition by the R.S.P.C.A. I was acutely embarrassed by the ceremony but delighted to get my hands on this vast amount of money.

Friday 3rd November Mr Haysman had me in his office this morning to congratulate me and offer financial guidance; after school I followed his advice and opened an account with the Post Office savings bank and celebrated with a visit to the Broadway cinema to see "Jesse James".

Sunday 5th November Two months into the war and on a sunny crisp morning I cycled to Baldock and there in a meadow at the junction of Norton Road and Hitchin Street I had my first sight of wartime

military activity, where behind a screen of elm trees a company of
soldiers with their tanks had halted. The tanks were a disappointment,
puny machines scarcely bigger than a saloon car and armed with a
solitary machine gun in a tiny turret. The troops belonged to an old
cavalry regiment and still wore the riding breeches, boots and burnished
spurs of their horse mounted days; these caused considerable danger and
embarrassment to their comrades as they clambered through the
armoured hatches into the tank's cramped interiors, evoking curses as
spurs encountered cloth and flesh. The Officers' batmen had obviously
worked wonders, as the polished jackboots, Sam Browne belts and well
pressed tunics of their masters testified, but I had a nagging suspicion
that they had learned nothing from the horrific slaughter of the first
World War and yearned to abandon the new fangled tanks for the
excitement of the charge with lance and sabre: certainly their little
tanks would be no match for the massive armoured monsters we saw on
the cinema newsreels parading before Hitler, and it was unlikely that
the Nazi tanks were commanded by fox hunting gentlemen.

My friends, Jack Taylor, Brian Peters, Russell Rogers and myself were
all avid readers of a newly published children's popular science
magazine, "Modern Wonder", which predicted space rockets of the
future, coloured illustrations of giant optical telescopes and the latest
details of the performance and armament of Allied and Nazi fighters
and bomber aircraft. We discussed endlessly the merits of the Hurricane
and the Messerschmitt, the Heinkel and the Blenheim and compared
the relative ranges and rates of fire of the Browning .303 machine gun
and the German 20mm cannon: why, we wondered did spies risk their
lives when the information was all there in the pages of "Modern
Wonder".

Meantime, we four friends aimlessly patrolled the Norton hedgerows
and spinneys with Russell's air rifle, firing at tin cans and murdering the
small birds; after all, if governments and clergy condoned the shooting
of people, who would condemn us for shooting sparrows?

Saturday 25th November Cycled into town this morning to buy Christmas cards and in the afternoon saw "Beau Geste" at the Broadway.

Monday 27th November Our afternoons of boredom ended abruptly when Mr Haysman and his staff finally devised a timetable which ensured fulltime schooling for ourselves and the London evacuees and peace for the hedgerow sparrows.

Thursday 30th November My diary notes: the weather was dull, we senior boys practised sword dancing at school, and the Red Army attacked Finland.

Saturday 2nd December A brief moment of excitement when a haystack in the field at the rear of our house caught fire, making a mockery of the blackout regulations. Letchworth Fire Brigade's magnificent new fire engine trundled up the deeply rutted Icknield Way and made valiant efforts to extinguish it, but through the night and all the next day it continued to smoulder and flare up.

Thursday 7th December My fourteenth birthday was rapidly approaching and with it the end of my school days; my form teacher, Mr Youngman, hinted that a career in journalism might suit me and gave me a job advertisement for a junior post on our local paper, but Dad was quite adamant that engineering offered a better future for me, and in the evening he gave me a job application form for Vauxhall Motors.

Monday 11th December I applied for a reference at school and the following day Mr Haysman gave me a fine testimonial which was posted with my application form at the weekend.

Thursday 14th December The Nazi "Graf Spee" was engaged by Royal Navy warships in the South Atlantic.

Monday 18th December Received news of the scuttling of the "Graf Spee" in South American waters; tonight we gathered around our radio to hear the First Sea Lord, Mr Churchill, congratulate the victors of the Battle of the River Plate.

Wednesday 20th December With Christmas approaching greetings cards and presents were bought and today the school term ended with the usual exchange of cards posted over several days in our improvised letter box which stood in the far corner of the classroom and whose contents would reveal who harboured a secret passion for whom. It was also the season for schoolboy pranks inflicted on our teachers on the only day in the long year when this was tolerated; a bottle of coloured liquid, labelled "hair restorer", encased in seasonal wrapping paper was sent to the bald Mr Poppy who only the day before had entranced us with his customary reading of "A Christmas Carol". Mr Poppy thanked us politely and beamed upon us with all the radiance of old Fezziwig, whilst Bernard Youngman, our form teacher, took leave of those of our classmates who were leaving school for the world of work with cordial wishes and handshakes.

Thursday 21st December Cycled up Lanark Hill to Weston village with my friend Jack Taylor to gather the holly.

Saturday 23rd December was the third day of hard frost and my fourteenth birthday; cycled down to the River Ivel at Norton Mill in the freezing fog and tonight celebrated with ginger beer and a family game of Monopoly.

Sunday 24th December A fine frosty Christmas eve and Ivor, Dad and I walked via Norton Mill and the Great North Road to Baldock; we put up the decorations and holly this evening and ate nuts sitting around the fire.

Monday 25th December We had turkey for Christmas, a rare luxury in those days and the last we were to enjoy for many years to come. The weather was a model of traditional Christmas; bitterly cold, the sun shining through fog and illuminating the frost encrusted trees: but no glowing lamps alight in windows welcomed our homecomings, no cheerful shop window displays or twinkling Christmas trees, only the stifling, all engulfing blackout and the white bands painted on lampposts and tree trunks in a vain attempt to prevent painful blunders in the blackness.

The Salvation Army band played carols with freezing fingers in Green Lane on Christmas morning and we sat down to enjoy our dinner of roasted turkey, mounds of sage, onion and bread stuffing and our mother's special plum pudding, made from her precious store of dried fruit and suet and boiled all day long in our kitchen copper as was her custom in the first week of October. She had also baked a Christmas cake at the same time "to give it time to come again": father called it "spice cake" and savoured it in the traditional Yorkshire fashion, accompanied by a crumbly piece of prime Cheshire cheese purchased at Moss and Sons – the grocers in Leys Avenue.

In the evening we all walked the two miles to the home of our sister Clarice's friend Grace Flack in Bursland; Grace was now Mrs Northwood and her husband Owen was with the Army in France and destined to be severely wounded in the Dunkirk disaster six months later. She was no doubt feeling rather sad to be separated from Owen at Christmas but soon cheered up over the mince pies and ginger wine and laughed with us at the Gracie Fields concert on the radio.

For the next few days it was possible to delude oneself that the war was all a bad dream; very little had happened in the past four months and there seemed no reason to suppose anything would. Idiotic "humorous" songs, "We're going to hang out the washing on the Siegfried Line" and "Run rabbit run" were ground out daily on the radio, whilst the "Kentucky Minstrels" helped uplift our spirits on the evening of Boxing Day.

The frost and snow continued for the rest of the week; Jack Taylor and I saw "Dodge City" at the Broadway cinema and together with Russell Rogers we spent hours sliding on the frozen Norton pond and hurling snowballs at each other and every passing target; one of my snowballs flung at Russell in Church Lane missed him and broke a kitchen window, much to the annoyance of his kindly mother.

Thursday 28th December Since I had passed my fourteenth birthday and was not in a paid job, I found myself a member of the army of the unemployed and was required to "sign on" at the Labour Exchange in Eastcheap today and every Thursday thereafter, a procedure both tedious and humiliating.

CHAPTER TWO

A long bitter winter

January–April 1940

Blizzards and burst pipes A magical Spring
Peter's death "Phoney war" ends Denmark invaded
Our family on the move

Tuesday, 2nd January Cycled through Baldock, Weston and Willian with Jack in fine frosty weather and walked across the frozen Weston pond.

Saturday 6th January We listened to "Garrison Theatre" on the radio.

Sunday 7th January Thick fog persists, the air raid sirens were tested this morning, reminding us that the war, after all, was a reality.

Wednesday 17th January Our hot water pipe was frozen.

Thursday 18th January The pipes are still solid and our radio set is broken.

Friday 19th January A great deal of snowballing at school. There was a great explosion at Waltham Abbey yesterday.

Sunday 28th January Very heavy fall of snow last night. Snowing most of the day and tonight. During January we experienced the most vile weather with frost, fog, snow and intermittent thaw, culminating in

Workmen erecting steel plate camouflage screens on P Block, many acres of which were soon in place, covering buildings, roadways and vehicle parking sites.

a terrible blizzard on this, the last weekend of the month. Father, who travelled daily to work at the Vauxhall factory in Luton, was stranded on Monday night when the bus became stuck on Offley Hill and again on Tuesday when the road to Hitchin and Letchworth was still blocked by huge snowdrifts, but finally managed to get home late on Wednesday night.

Since September Vauxhall had been engaged in a race to equip our long neglected army with trucks and other munitions of war. Father was becoming exhausted and short tempered by the long hours of work and the daily twenty mile round journeys; the previous weekend had produced evidence of this when a dispute over a trivial and long forgotten matter resulted in a literally "blazing row" between our parents when a cushion was flung onto the fire and burned.

The bitter weather persisted through February and intermittently into March; the sole heating in our house, like most others, was a single

The northern side of P Block in the winter of 1939/40 with 15 cwt. MW army trucks awaiting dispatch.

open fire in the living room and frozen water pipes were the inevitable result of a frosty winter; twice our father thawed them out with rags soaked in hot water, but in mid March a torrent spurted from under the kitchen sink and the plumber was sent for to staunch the flood with his blowlamp and moleskin glove and to seal the split pipe with molten lead.

Friday 1st March Peter Duncombe, the young brother of our friend Roy, was badly injured yesterday evening when he fell from an old elm tree which stood in the hedge bordering "the highway", the ancient Icknield Way to Baldock, and was operated on today for a ruptured kidney at Fairfield hospital.

Saturday 2nd March Went to town on an errand for Mr Duncombe; Peter is seriously ill.

Sunday 3rd March Mrs Duncombe told mother that Peter "passed away" this morning. We celebrated Ivor's thirteenth birthday with a special tea; a beautiful sunny day.

Friday 8th March Peter was brought home last night to rest in his coffin in the front room: Mum bought flowers for the funeral.

Saturday 9th March Took flowers to the Duncombe's house in Temple Gardens this morning: Mrs Duncombe invited me in for a last look at Peter; it was the first corpse I had seen but to me it resembled a china doll and in no way had any likeness to the living boy I knew. We all attended the funeral at Willbury cemetery this afternoon.

Wednesday 13th March It snowed most of the day to a depth of 2 inches, the roads are very bad; plumber mended the water pipe.

Saturday 16th March Saw Deanna Durbin in "First Love" at the Broadway cinema this afternoon.

Thursday 21st March Cycled to Hitchin with Jack Taylor and Jim Wright this morning where we viewed the tiny church museum in a room over the south porch. Saw "Shipyard Sally" at Baldock cinema tonight and got back late.

Easter Monday 25th March By Easter the bitter Winter finally relented and on Easter Monday Ivor and I cycled through Baldock and Clothall to the lovely village of Cottered, where great drifts of daffodils spread across the village green and the newly budded hawthorn cast a haze of green over the hedgerows.

Friday 29th March Called at the Labour Exchange in Eastcheap and tried to get a temporary job at W H Smiths; cycled to Baldock with

A horse drawn cart and a Bedford lorry on Vauxhall Road pass the western end of H Block press shop: the hillside allotments on the right conceal air raid trenches dug by Vauxhall volunteers 18 months earlier.

Jack Taylor this afternoon and saw Royal Artillery field guns drawn up in the High Street.

Sunday 31st March Jack and I walked to Norton Bury, across the fields to Black Horse farm where the tall reed beds were a favourite bird nesting site for us. The grieving Mrs Duncombe visited us in the evening for a comforting chat with Mum and Dad.

Monday 1st April was the final day of our Easter school holiday and Jack and I cycled to Weston village to gaze with awe upon the grave of our legendary local "Robin Hood", the giant outlaw and master archer known as "Jack-o-Legs". His bones we were assured rested in Weston churchyard where his last arrow stuck in the turf after flying three miles from the site of his execution at Baldock: a folk hero and friend of the poor, he is commemorated by "Jack's Hill" on the Great North Road where he robbed wealthy travellers.

Tuesday 2nd April Back to school today and began to read "Dombey and Son": weather fine – showers at times.

Friday 5th April Ivor has a black eye. Mum mended my trousers tonight.

Sunday 7th April Cycled through Henlow and Shefford to Old Warden this morning; it was the most beautiful village I have ever seen and inspired me to spend some time sketching one of the lodges at the entrance to the estate. Whether the war made us aware of our mortality, or after the Winter with its seemingly endless frosts and smothering

The approach road to a camouflaged V Block and a few of the many hundreds of finished and partly finished army trucks which crowded every road and spare piece of ground.

X and V Blocks seen from the filter beds of Luton sewage works – later the site of the postwar AA Block. In the air raid of 30th August twenty three bombs fell on the sewage works and the explosions threw a foul-smelling coating of clinker and raw sewage onto the walls of K Block adjoining Eaton Green road. Steel mesh camouflage shapes can be seen on X Block's roof; these were intended to disguise the angular lines of the building.

blackout induced in us all a black mood, the onset of Spring roused the spirits and set Ivor, Jack and myself upon a quest for sweet violets in the hedge bottoms and the tender new shoots of nettles to take home for mother to make broth: a tasty country remedy which she claimed "cleansed the blood". Father, who had commuted to his job at Vauxhall's plant in Luton for seven years and suffered the strain of travelling daily by bus through that dreadful winter, finally agreed with mother that the family should find a new home in Luton; brother Ivor was to leave Letchworth Grammar School and transfer to Luton's Technical College and Vauxhall was to be reminded of my job application.

Change was in the air: mother and sister Clarice searched Luton for a suitable house to rent and in spare moments disused furniture and rubbish from the garden sheds and henhouses was burned in the garden.

Tuesday 9th April It was not only the Hardisty family however that was on the move: two weeks after Easter Hitler's troops invaded Denmark, ending the long stalemate of the "phoney war", an explosion of violence which revealed the awesome power of the Nazi war machine and the fate which awaited the rest of Europe. So swift was the attack there was no time to move the flags on my Daily Telegraph war map and, in any case, I lost interest; war was not a game after all.

Monday 15th April The Culvert School from Tottenham, which had shared our classrooms since the previous September, formally merged with our school, and my job application finally bore fruit when I received a letter from Vauxhall Motors requiring me to come for an interview tomorrow morning.

The Spring weather had turned cold with showers of hail and sleet, but Spring was not to be denied and, in the evening, I discovered a blackbird's nest with a clutch of eggs. "Chopped wood tonight for our fire because coal is running short".

CHAPTER THREE

Vauxhall — first impressions

April–June 1940

Vauxhall interview – Mr Johnson's advice
Getting to know Norman, Trevor and Arthur
A warning from "the Skipper"   First pay packet
Sergeant Simpson, "Fanny" Farlow and "Bronco Bill"
We move to Devon Road   Chamberlain out – Churchill in
Last troops escape Dunkirk
"Lord Haw Haw" gloats, Churchill hurls defiance
Planning records staff photographed for posterity

Tuesday 16th April I travelled by bus to Luton to attend interview
with Mr Johnson, the Manager of the Tool Planning Department in X
Block.

Mr Johnson was a short rotund man who smoked a pipe constantly
and exuded an aura of calmness and quiet efficiency: he was in
conference with his deputy Mr Thursby when I arrived and I had to
wait some minutes nervously perched on a chair in his secretary's office
before he could see me.

My interview was brief and to the point; he studied my school
references which spoke flatteringly of my artistic abilities and
draughtsmanship and he asked me whether I was prepared to study two
or three nights a week at Luton's Technical College for 2 years until I
was sixteen and then apply for admission to Vauxhall's Apprentice
School. Grammar School boys applied on leaving school at sixteen, but

the rest of us had to tread a harder path; two years fetching and carrying, running errands and performing any and every menial task. Office boys were at everyone's beck and call, the lowest of the low and regarded by the other staff as "dogsbodies", but at least it was a toehold, a small step towards adulthood and my weekly wage would be an improvement on the one shilling and sixpence I had earned on Saturdays working nine hours for a tight fisted greengrocer and would be a welcome addition to the family budget.

Thursday 18th April A letter arrived addressed to Master O. Hardisty from S. T. Lewis, Office Manager, Vauxhall Motors Ltd; "we confirm that we have decided to engage you as Office Boy in our Planning Department at the salary of 12/6d (twelve shillings and sixpence) per week plus 2/- War Bonus. We shall be glad if you will confirm by return that you can commence your duties here at 9 a m on Monday the 22nd inst. Reporting to Mr Morris. The normal office hours are from 9 a m to 5.30 p m – 12 noon on Saturdays". The following day I said my farewells to my form teacher and headmaster, Mr Haysman, and at 4 o'clock walked through the school gates for the last time with mixed feelings of excitement and apprehension. Since my fourteenth birthday at Christmas I had been officially unemployed, a shameful status which required weekly visits to the Labour Exchange to "sign on", but now, freed from this humiliating impediment, I joyfully handed in my card and received the good wishes of the clerk.

Dad woke me at dawn on Monday, 22nd April, and with shoes polished and hair slicked down, I walked with him in the chill early morning sunshine past the Bacon factory and the Gasworks to the bus stop where at half past six we boarded the Vauxhall workmen's bus.

Up the stairs to the upper deck thick with tobacco smoke and the sour smell of machinists' cutting oil which clung to boots and clothing and which was soon to be become so familiar. More men boarded the bus at the Midland Bank and still more in Hitchin before the bus

Vauxhall Motors Ltd

| TELEPHONE
NUMBER 2600 LUTON | LUTON. | BEDS. | TELEGRAMS
CARVAUX. TELEX. LUTON |

WHEN REPLYING PLEASE QUOTE
→ OUR REF: 202/STL/EA

YOUR REF:

17th April 1940.

Master O. Hardisty,
74 Green Lane,
LETCHWORTH,
Herts..

Dear Sir,

      With reference to your interview here on the 16th inst., we confirm that we have decided to engage you as Office Boy in our Planning Department at the salary of 12/6d. (twelve shillings and six pence) per week plus 2/-d. War Bonus.

      We shall be glad if you will confirm by return that you can commence your duties here at 9 am. on Monday, the 22nd inst., reporting to Mr. Morris. The normal office hours are from 9 am. until 5.30 pm; 12 noon on Saturdays.

      We are enclosing with this letter details of the various Welfare Schemes at present in operation, and would advise you to carefully peruse these.

      Please complete and return the card referring to the Life Assurance Scheme, and bring your National Health and Unemployment cards with you.

Yours faithfully,
VAUXHALL MOTORS LIMITED.

S.T. LEWIS,
Office Manager.

enc.

TURN OVER FOR CONDITIONS OF EMPLOYMENT.

crossed the Market Square, down Sun Street and climbed the slope of Tilehouse Street. We ground slowly through the beeches of Offley Hill to pick up more passengers waiting by the village pond and then by Stopsley and Round Green to Luton and Vauxhall's W Block gate in Kimpton Road.

Even at this early hour, Kimpton Road was filled with a mass of moving humanity, with thousands disgorging from buses and other thousands on bicycles and on foot hurrying to "clock on".

A gaunt faced man wearing a trilby hat stood by the factory gate selling newspapers from a child's perambulator; my father greeted him and bought a paper and, as we toiled up the hill towards V Block, he told me that this man was Wally Plumb, whose brother Fred had been killed at Jarama in Spain three years before, fighting against Hitler's ally General Franco with the Republican International Brigade's British Battalion.

We fell in step with several of Dad's toolroom colleagues to whom he proudly introduced me and as we breasted the hill I saw through the morning haze the whole vast complex in the valley below; over Q Block to P Block and the huge vaulted roof of the Works canteen: beyond them K Block, the main office buildings and the distant bulk of H Block press shop. To the West, the older buildings by the railway where the engines were built and Y Block on the far side of the rail tracks and now under construction, destined soon to be the Churchill tank shop. Vauxhall was by this time on a thorough war footing, a major supplier of vehicles and munitions to our armed forces and for this reason every effort had been made to hide or disguise the buildings, as it was certain to be a prime target for Nazi bombers. False profiles on the rooftops and acre upon acre of wire netting covered with thousands of steel plates were suspended from walls and frames of steel girders; the whole vast screen and the buildings underneath painted in shades of green, grey, black and brown.

Hundreds of finished and partly finished lorries in the same dreary camouflage were parked under these canopies and an overpowering stench of paint, lubricants and rubber filled the air; I thought wistfully of my recent idle school days and was overwhelmed by feelings of awe and bewilderment.

Office staff commenced work a full hour after the manual workers, so there was time for me to be introduced to father's fellow toolmakers and their foreman Bert Gibbs, a fiery little man and possessor of a waxed moustache, an exotic vocabulary and a notoriously short temper. My father had served his time in the great engineering works of Leeds in Victorian days; he was a craft Union man of the old school, intensely proud of his skill and, like Bert Gibbs, well known for his explosive reactions, especially when he thought his ability as a craftsman had been impugned. He had a glass eye, the result of an accident at work, and when angry his good eye would glare with a terrible ferocity: I later learned of a monumental flare up between Dad and Bert Gibbs which had entered the annals of toolroom folklore but of which I then knew nothing.

The toolmakers' benches lined a balcony which overlooked the cavernous echoing space of the die shop, with its huge machines and overhead travelling cranes where the dies were made and then hauled at snail's pace on a multi-wheeled trailer to the press shop half a mile distant.

Windows and glass skylights had long been obscured by layers of opaque paint, the only light coming from hundreds of electric lamps suspended in the dark void and the only daylight entering where the big doors at the end of the shop stood open, with the emergency ambulance permanently parked ready for use.

In a corner of the die shop stood a large machine of Swiss manufacture which Dad explained was a jig borer and which was operated by Jack Leovold, a tall thin man with ginger hair. I was introduced to Jack, and then Dad took great care to impress upon me the incredible precision of this machine which was capable of producing work to an accuracy of one ten thousandth of an inch. He obviously had great respect for Jack and the enormous responsibility he carried, where one tiny mistake could result in the ruin of a precision jig worth thousands of pounds.

As nine o'clock approached I made my way to the Planning Records Office where I reported with some trepidation to Mr Norman Morris, the supervisor, who sat at his desk like a Sultan with a harem of ten lady typists whose desks ranged in two rows in front of him: he indicated the desk I was to occupy, which was situated in front of the typists and slightly to the side so that he could keep his eye on me at all times.

Mr Morris was a portly, bespectacled gentleman with a tightly-pursed mouth and wearing a light grey suit. He strode about purposefully, exuding an air of importance, and in my mind resembled a stately battleship sailing into action. Like Mr Johnson, he admonished me to enrol for night school and introduced me to his deputy Bert Waller and his clerk Arthur Fulcher whose job it was to issue drawings and blueprints to the die design draughtsmen and whom I was to assist whenever I had spare time on my hands. I was then placed under the tutelage of Trevor Dean, a neatly dressed, patient young man whose duties I was to learn and take over in the week or so before he was liberated, having passed his sixteenth birthday, to join the Apprentice School lads in P Block.

Trevor was eager to pass on his burden and in no time at all he introduced me to the mass of paperwork it would be my job to record and file: internal works orders, Government orders, purchase requisitions, operation sheets, tool orders and memorandums. They came in pink, green, blue and plain white, to be filed by date, E number, G number or part number. Before the morning was through I despaired that I would ever remember all these instructions, whereupon Trevor, with infinite patience, made notes for me in his neat, newly acquired draughtsman's script.

A padlocked "cubby hole" at the foot of the stairwell in the Block's main entrance housed our stationery store and a heavy tradesman's bike with a large carrier basket and Planning Records Dept. X Block on a plate fixed under the crossbar. Its punctured tyres and general upkeep were my responsibility, but for major repairs and routine servicing I had to take it to the New Hudson Cycle Company, otherwise known as Partridge's in Chapel Street. Stored also with the bike, for my comfort in inclement weather, was a voluminous yellow oilskin cape, waterproof leggings and a quaint hat of the style worn by Victorian lifeboatmen as depicted in advertisements for "Fishermen's Friend" throat lozenges. However, the comical effect of donning this outmoded garb was so great that I often preferred to endure the rain rather than the jeers and laughter, the cries of "abandon ship" or "hello sailor" from my fellow office boys.

Another of my duties was to collect stationery supplies from the stores which were located down a steep ramp leading from Kimpton Road into a dark basement under K Block offices, and there to load the bike's carrier with all the supplies needed for the drawing offices; five foot rolls of cartridge paper, typing paper, Indian ink, pencils and tracing linen, and push the heavy load up the half mile slope to X Block. The subterranean location also concealed one of Vauxhall's strangest operations; it was the site of the plant's mailing department, its communications centre, where a staff of twenty or so young boys and girls collected, sorted and despatched all the internal and external mail. The captain of this high spirited crew was Miss Farlow, an ample lady of ferocious reputation who was referred to – out of earshot – as "Fanny Farlow". The sight of these cheeky urchins in their lair, scurrying back and forth on their errands, created a Dickensian image akin to Fagin's kitchen. All around the plant they could be seen, in workshop, office and roadway, with heavy mail bags slung from their shoulders: one of their number, Dennis Orchard, I often encountered as we pushed our bikes together up the hill to V Block, where in the entrance he and six others were destined to meet their death four months hence when a

Nazi bomb crashed through the stairwell.

I soon discovered that a considerable hazard for office boys on bicycles were the scores of small motorised runabouts employed by the material handling division which sped around the plant laden with raw material and components; many of these were manufactured by the Leeds firm Greenwood and Batley and were known as "Greenbats", whilst the rest were supplied in pre-war years by General Motors' German arm, Adam Opel, now producing munitions for Hitler, but German or British they were all "Greenbats" to Vauxhall workers.

Another hazard were the big Fordson tractors used by the Plant maintenance division to haul heavy machinery; the driver of one particular tractor was a lanky, unwashed character who wore a trilby hat and was reputed to live in a cottage at East Hyde. He was nicknamed "Bronco Bill" due to his habit of bouncing on the sprung driver's seat in time with the tractor's motion, and in hot weather it was his custom to remove his trilby and hang it on the top of the tractor's vertical exhaust pipe, where the hat's interior was soon fumigated by the products of combustion, so that, even without his hat, Bronco could easily be recognised by the ring of soot around his hairline.

The Vauxhall factory was sited on what had been hilly farmland on the Eastern flank of the Lea Valley and its construction had involved the excavation of millions of tons of chalk, much of which was dumped in huge spoil heaps on St Anne's Hill behind X and V Blocks. The result of this unsuitable terrain was that blocks W, V, X and Q were situated on considerably higher levels than blocks A, B, J. P, K, H and G and all the older blocks flanking the Western side of Kimpton Road and the new Y block tank shop beyond the railway. From the vantage point of the plant entrance gate on St Anne's Hill the view over the roof tops to the South was down the Lea Valley towards Harpenden and London some thirty miles distant, with the main line to St Pancras crawling along the valley floor. On the valley's distant western side, the wooded acres of Luton Hoo nudged Vauxhall's boundary, whilst the fledgling

Luton Airport and the grim red brick Spitalsea Isolation Hospital dominated the skyline on the plateau to the East.

Working in the offices, I soon discovered, was hot and claustrophobic due to the total blackout requiring all skylights to be covered and all windows fitted with shutters, so only those lucky enough to work near the open shutters could enjoy fresh air and daylight, otherwise everyone worked by electric light however hot and sunny the day outside.

To escape into the open air was a great relief and I eagerly followed Trevor on his internal mail delivery round; every Area Manager, General foreman and foreman had his own route number to which items were addressed and I had to learn by rote, names, route numbers and locations in the plant. It was a great opportunity to explore the factory and acquaint myself with its strange sights and teeming workshops. I became familiar with the mighty presses booming in the dim vastness of the Press shop, the flickering lighting of the arc welding booths and the relentlessly moving track assembly line in K Block: but the strangest of all to my young mind was the Bar Shop in the underground basement of P Block, where even in peacetime daylight never penetrated and where lines of automatic bar lathes chattered away night and day, as the operators stood on wooden duck boards clad in long rubber aprons to protect them from the foul smelling, lard cutting oil which splashed everywhere and formed sullen pools under the boards, or the heat treatment shops where glowing furnaces roared and oil quenching tanks briefly spouted yellow flame and vats of red hot cyanide bubbled and spat like the vent holes of a volcano.

Trevor led me through the main office entrance where the Vauxhall Griffin emblem carved in stone hovered over the door, past the Chief Commissionaire, Sergeant Simpson, whose little office was just inside the entrance, and up the panelled staircase to the cashier's office where I would be sent to cash cheques for our department's managers on their frequent trips to the Midlands and the North.

Members of the Corps of Commissionaires manned every factory gate and the entrance door to every major Block; each of them was a pensioned ex-serviceman clad in a uniform with peaked cap, polished boots and patent leather cross belt, who deferred to Company executives and important visitors and treated everyone else with polite disdain: their chief, Sergeant Simpson, was a ramrod backed, flint faced old soldier with a much be-medalled chest and a gimlet eye which missed nothing; usually office boys were beneath his notice, but from time to time he would acknowledge me with a slight nod.

Vauxhall's wages at this time were paid in cash, and every Thursday morning the big Company limousine, with chauffeur, cashier and Sergeant Simpson sitting stiffly in the rear seat, would collect the money from a bank in town. On one memorable occasion, I passed through the main entrance when the Sergeant was preparing to leave for the weekly cash run and was busy holstering a large revolver under his tunic. I saw the Chief Commissionaire in a new light thereafter; anyone prepared to risk his life to guard my fourteen shillings and sixpence was worthy of my respect.

Thursday 25th April I ventured into the main canteen to eat my packed sandwiches; it had a vaulted roof where echoes lingered and which reminded me of a smaller version of St Pancras station with a large stage and proscenium arch filling one end. Thousands of overalled workers sat at the tables or queued at the serving counters, whilst the Vauxhall Concert Orchestra conducted by Mr Fred Green battled with the terrible acoustics and the din of the feeding multitude to grind out "Roll out the Barrel", "South of the Border" or "Begin the Beguine".

Friday 26th April was a memorable day when Mr Morris brought round a tray laden with small manilla envelopes containing our wages; my packet contained a ten shilling note, a few coins and a leaflet from our Managing Director, Mr Charles Bartlett, entitled "A note on Present Conditions". After outlining the problems of maintaining

A NOTE ON PRESENT CONDITIONS

I FEEL that a few thoughts on our present circumstances might be interesting and helpful, although I am sure you will appreciate that there are many things we cannot discuss very well at the present time.

First of all, you will like to know that the work which we have been able to do for the Government has been very highly appreciated, and that we have certainly been able to " do our bit " as we said we would. Everybody has tackled the job wonderfully, and in spite of all the material difficulties and disruption caused by war conditions, we have maintained our production and our productive capacity in a way that has brought us the warmest commendation.

We on the management side appreciate what our men have done very much indeed, for conditions of working are difficult and the maintenance of output in these conditions of blackout and so on has been very remarkable.

These blackout conditions are a very great problem to the Management, and we have got to try and do everything possible to improve conditions by better lighting, better ventilation and whatever else we can do to make the lives of our people as decent as we can under these stringent regulations. This we will do, and the whole subject is being investigated to see what can be done to get the best working conditions that we can, consistent with the rules that govern us just now.

A warning from the "Skipper" Charles Bartlett. "If we get an alarm move quickly and orderly to your trenches or to your post. But move quickly." 25th April 1940.

production and thanking the workforce for their efforts, he apologised for the working conditions and promised the management would do everything possible to improve lighting and ventilation; and then ominously: "one small word about air raid alarms. We feel we have done as much as we can with practice dispersal etc., since after two or three practice dispersals nobody hurries anymore! So now we must leave it largely to you, individually, to do the best you can. If we get an alarm, move, quickly and orderly to your trenches or to your post. But move quickly for the saving of life may depend on how quickly we can get out of sight with all large scale movement stopped and hidden".

That Friday was also memorable for Mr Morris, being the twenty first anniversary of his starting at Vauxhall, so after handing out our pay packets, he brought round a celebratory tray of fancy cakes; one for everyone, not forgetting the office boys.

Saturday 27th April It was Mum's fifty-third birthday today and we marked it with a modest tea. Saw "Sons of the Sea" at the Broadway Cinema tonight.

Sunday 28th April A glorious sunny day. Jack and I wandered along the banks of the river Ivel this morning. Returned to Nortonbury and the Ivel this evening with sister Clarice and gathered bunches of cowslips on the water meadows.

It was a time for farewells; our family was to move to Luton in the coming week, so that weekend and several evenings following were spent in sad reflective mood and vowing to keep in touch with school mates and neighbours.

Wednesday 1st May The eve of our departure and I called on Jack Taylor and Russell Rogers, then sister Clarice, brother Ivor and myself joined our parents in the frantic preparations for the morning's move, bagging and boxing our possessions late into the night.

A 1939 aerial photograph taken from a point over Powdrill's farm in Crawley Green Road. Most of the Vauxhall plant is in view with X,V,Q,P and W Blocks in the mid-field; the circular skid test pan on the left and the recently built St. Annes estate in the foreground with the houses in Durham Road, Norfolk Road, Rutland Crescent and Devon Road, clearly seen.

Thursday 2nd May Our family left Letchworth and our home at Number 74 Green Lane and I crossed the railway bridge and boarded the early morning Vauxhall works bus in Works Road for the last time. At lunchtime I ventured once more to the canteen to eat my sandwiches, as the Vauxhall orchestra gave their regular Thursday concert, and at half past five I climbed the steep path at the rear of X Block to join the family at our new home at 9 Devon Road, a semi-detached house with a small garden.

Dad and Jim Barlass, a Scot and fellow toolmaker who lived in nearby Norfolk Road, erected our garden shed with a little help from me, and I later wandered round the estate to explore our surroundings and ponder on my new circumstances. My first impression was the lack of space compared with our home in Letchworth; no tree lined streets here and no open country on our doorstep. The St Anne's estate had been built a few years previously on land which had been part of the adjoining Powdrill's Farm, and our house was less than a hundred yards from Vauxhall's boundary fence and within a ten minute walk of our workplace in X Block, so that, even to a fourteen year old boy, it was obvious that a major Nazi air raid on the plant would put our home and the entire St Anne's estate in great peril. Vauxhall's workforce at this time was almost entirely male, with a high proportion coming from Scotland, South Wales and the North of England during the years of the great depression where the old industries were collapsing and the people were suffering terrible privation and even starvation. Many had joined the numerous "hunger marches" to Parliament or had been directed by their local Labour Exchanges or Trade Unions to areas in the South like Luton, Dagenham or Oxford, where new industries were taking on labour and where they now rejoiced in the incredible luxury of a regular wage packet, even though the work was monotonous to the point of distraction. Female employees were restricted to traditional "women's jobs", secretarial and office work, catering and cleaning, but within twelve months, all was to be transformed and old prejudices shaken to their foundations as thousands of men were called up to the armed forces and an army of women, hastily trained and organised by Ernie Bevin's Ministry of Labour, were drafted into Vauxhall's assembly lines and workshops.

Our immediate neighbours were all Vauxhall workers, Jack Hardy and Arthur Boughey, production machinists, and Lloyd (Bill) Creighton, a "Geordie" diemaker, who, like Dad and I, worked in X

right No one had ever heard of fitted kitchens and double glazing in 1940 – the "must have" home improvement was a decent, solid concrete or steel air raid shelter.

BEHIND THE DOOR (A)

WELLINGTON CINEMA

GRANDPA GOES TO TOWN (U)

Don't come Saturday if you can come before

DOROTHY LAMOUR & ROBERT PRESTON in **TYPHOON** (U)

Also WILLIAM BOYD in **RANGE WAR** (U)

OPEN DAILY FROM 7 P.M.

WHILE STOCKS LAST

AIR RAID SHELTERS

IN 12 GAUGE GALVANISED

CORRUGATED IRON
'also in CONCRETE

IMMEDIATE DELIVERY

EX STOCK

GIBBS and DANDY LTD
34, GEORGE STREET, LUTON

" ...and we're helping, too."

Fighting hard, working hard, paying hard. The men and women of Britain are doing it gladly.

But the children won't be left out of it. They're helping, too. Young legs are strong legs, and tiredness doesn't matter. They are working with a will for their country and they're finding something they can do.

Every week a small boy or girl may come to your door. They are collecting old newspapers and magazines. All they get they take to school and the school bundles it up and sells it. The school does what it likes with the money, but a lot of it comes back to the Red Cross, and now there's a big drive on to help buy a Spitfire.

So help the children on with their collections, please. Give them all the old newspapers and magazines you've got. They are Waste Paper Collectors and they're helping Britain to win the war.

SALVAGED LOSTS

The Emergency Committee having changed the weekly pay day for A.R.P. whole-time employees from Friday to Wednesday, the Council agreed to the pay day for all weekly-paid employees being changed from Friday to some other weekday as be fixed by the Chairman of the Finance Committee and the Borough Treasurer.

SEWER LOAN APPROVED

The Ministry of Health wrote consenting to a loan for construction of the Vauxhall outfall sewer, less the agreed contribution by Vauxhall Motors, Ltd., of two-thirds of the additional cost entailed by altering the line of the sewer up to a maximum of £11,500.

The Borough Engineer reported that it would be necessary to make experimental bore-holes, and was authorised to do this at a cost not exceeding £150.

LEAGRAVE HOUSING ESTATE

The Council agreed that "Pirton-road" be suggested to the Street Names Sub-committee for a new street of the Leagrave Housing Estate.

It was also decided to approach the Ministry of Health to ascertain the possibility of building the remaining 22 houses on that Estate.

SIGNS OF THE SEASON

It was agreed that 500 pairs of woollen gloves should be bought from a Derby firm at a cost of £81 5s., and that uniforms for 37 special constables be bought from the same firm for £201 19s. 2d.

A second greatcoat for members of the police war reserve was approved, and two firms are to be asked to quote.

SLAUGHTERHOUSE LICENCES

The Public Health Committee reported having received a deputation from Luton and District Retail Butchers' Association. The Association Secretary read a statement setting out their views on the Council's action in refusing to grant certain slaughterhouse licences.

The statement was received.

REMEMBRANCE SERVICE

The Rev. W. Curry, on behalf of the Free Church Council, wrote inviting the Corporation and officials to attend the United Remembrance service at the Parish Church on lines similar to that of last year. Alderman Arnold moved that the invitation be accepted, and the Council agreed.

FOR SERVICES RENDERED

On the motion of Alderman Currant, the Council accorded thanks to the Chairmen of Committees for the able manner in which they had carried out their duties in the past year.

Proposing that similar thanks be accorded to co-opted members of committees and the voluntary lady workers at the welfare centres, the Mayor mentioned the resignation of Mrs. Smith from the Maternity and Child Welfare Committee, of Mr Alison Blundell from the Museum Sub-Committee and Mr. W W Merchant from the Education Committee.

Suggesting that the Council send a letter of appreciation to Mr. Merchant for his many services, he said, Mr. Merchant had been a member of the Education Committee for 32 years and had proved a genial, loyal and sincere colleague Councillor Peter Mitchell seconded and the motion was carried.

Members present were: The Mayor (Councillor J Burgoyne), the Deputy-Mayor Alderman C C Dillingham; Alderman A. E. Ansell, H Arnold, P W Currant, S H Godfrey, O E Hart, W F Mullett, A E Nicholls and G Wistow Walker Councillors G Bavister G Brooker, W J Edwards, P G Gladwell, W A Gregory, J Harrison, H S Hewson, Lady Keens, T H Knight, W J Lane, R Colin Large, H C Lawrence, Percy Mitchell, P E Mitchell, H C Os'ey, P J Randall A Richardson, W G Roberts, G F Seaward, A Sinfield, S Smith, S B J Snoxell, W G Veals, and P R Williams.

KIMPTON

CORN REPLACES FOOTBALL — The footboll pitch used by Kimpton F.C. who disbanded at the outbreak of war, has come under the plough. The field is being grown with wheat, after being grassland for about thirty years.

MORE MEN SERVING — Recent

Harpenden, was married penden Parish Church on Her bridegroom was Se Derrick E. Ingram T Durham Light Infantry, the late Mr Edward and of Mrs E F Pragnell o The bride's family, of wrecks ago, lived in London and moved to when their home was b Mr, C E Mander is adv director of the Amalgam and his son Mr S Ma a similar position with Pearson, Ltd.

Given away by her t bride wore a petrol blue trimmed with grey fur match. She carried bouquet of roses and whi fuchsia ensemble with a orchids Second-Lieut. L of the Bufts brother of was best man.

The mother of the bri black dress with cyclam sories, while Mrs. Pragn mustard-coloured dress w and hat.

The Rector, the Rev S conducted the service. choral. Dr A C Tysoe. Abbey organist, was at and the Parish Church augmented by two boy so the Abbey

The church was decor gold and bronze chrysant Many friends from the and publishing world and reception at the home of after which the new couple left for a hone Broadway, Worcester.

Car Left With Lights

A 13-years-old Harpende Bruce Atkins was fine Luton Borough Court on for failing to have lights on a stationary car at 7.50 p.m. on Septemb a further fine of 20s. wa on at same time and car War Reserves Elkins had left his car outside Theatre. While waiting f ness had to use a torch other cars from collid Atkins's car When he Atkins said he was sorr been so long.

Atkins, who wrote regret, said he was told it not necessary to have lig car at that spot.

Knock, Kno

Defendant: Can you why the summons was o to my back door?

Clerk: There is no re which governs to which summons should be de Defendant: Oh! I thought it had to be to the front door — Interlude at St Division Court on Satu

CLOPHILL

A WHIST DRIVE in a Spitfire Fund was held Schools on Friday. Mr was M.C., and presented to — Ladies, 1 Mrs 1 Hous N. Dunham; 3. Mrs. Kirby 1 Sgm Bent; 2. Mr C 3. Sgm Broderick Spe Guddin

SCOUTS' CINEMA — Ope the Scoutmaster. Mr L cinema visited Maulden a £2 is for the Spitfire Fun

MOTHERS' BRIGHT HO in the Methodist School Thursday, under the Mrs. Middleton. In the a Mr Tho'as, Mrs Selwood "Others." Mrs. Veals read CHRISTIAN ENDEAVO A Coleman opened the session of the Christian E in connection with the Chapel with the motto, good faith with faith" elected were : Mr H Abbe dent : Mr) A Harris. Mr A Matthews, treasu Matthews organist. Th meeting on Friday was le R Abbott

THE DEATH took p Sunday of Mr William J

Block. Bill, a passionate socialist, had served his time as a naval shipyard fitter on the Tyne and had a virulent hatred of Tory politicians who he blamed for his family's suffering in the great depression; the years had not abated his rage when he recalled their terrible poverty and the humiliation of the means test when every saleable household chattel was assessed before any relief was grudgingly given. He and our father (also known as Bill) had much in common; as fellow Northerners, fellow socialists and fellow craftsmen, they were never short of a topic of conversation and soon became firm friends. Almost two weeks into my new job and I was getting to know Arthur Fulcher, our print issue clerk, a slightly-built man of middle years and smartly turned out with polished boots and slicked down hair. His manner was formal and grave, but I sensed a carefully concealed sly sense of humour and a warmth and sympathy for the under-dog; in odd moments he told me of his boyhood in rural Norfolk, where the only alternative to scaring birds on the fields for five shillings a week was to enter "service".

He regaled me with tales of tyrannical butlers and housekeepers; of smuggling his drunken master and his friend the dissolute King Edward, known as "Dirty Bertie", through a side door of Buckingham Palace after their nights of debauchery in the West End: he told me that the British Officer class had the use of soldier servants, even when on active service, to maintain them in the style to which they were accustomed, and when the Great War broke out he enlisted – although he had little choice in the matter and accompanied his aristocratic master to France with the British Expeditionary Force where he spent a relatively comfortable war on the Western Front as his Lordship's batman.

Something that had nagged me for days finally dawned when I realised that Arthur, with his striped trousers, neat black jacket,

right DON'T PANIC! Regular siren tests were a fact of everyday life in the Spring and Summer of 1940.

AND TOY DEALER.
Also a Quantity of Useful
HOUSEHOLD FURNITURE, ETC.
To be Sold by Auction by

H. Holyoak & Son
On WEDNESDAY and THURSDAY,
APRIL 24th and 25th, 1940, at
ELEVEN O'CLOCK each day. By
Order of the Executor of the Late
MR. AMOS THOMPSON
Auction and Estate Offices, 33 Castle-
street, Luton

BEDS, HERTS & ADJOINING
COUNTIES

Frederick Reeks & Goode,
F.A.I.
Incorporating
R. O. HARDING HARPENDEN
Auctioneers Surveyors Valuers Land and
Estate Agents.
Auction Rooms: Vaughan-road Harpen-
den
Estate Offices: 10 King-street Luton
(Tel. 19.

Telephone: 41 Dunstable. Telegram:
Allcorn Dunstable.

STORE STOCK SALE.
DUNSTABLE CATTLE MARKET.

Mr. Chas. A. Allcorn, F.A.I.,
WILL hold the Annual Sale of STORE
CATTLE and SHEEP in the above
Market on FRIDAY, 26th APRIL, 1940,
at 1 o'clock.
Early entries should please be sent to
the Auctioneer, Dunstable.

Telephone 2030 Bedford and Abbey
3601
Telegrams—"Eve. B. dford."

Messrs. J. R. Eve & Son,
LAND AGENTS, SURVEYORS
AND AUCTIONEERS
Offices:
40, MILL STREET, BEDFORD,
BANCROFT, HITCHIN ('Phone
Hitchin 168), and
2 & 3, THE SANCTUARY,
WESTMINSTER, S.W.1

SOCIAL WELFARE OF TROOPS
FLAG DAY—9th MARCH, 1940

	£	s.	d.			£	s.	d.
Street Collections	386	15	2	Emblems		20	13	0
				Postage			19	3
				Advertising		1	9	3
				Balance		363	13	8
	£386	15	2			£386	15	2

Audited and found correct.
F. BUNTING,
Hon Treasurer.

FLORENCE E. BURGOYNE.
A. M. DILLINGHAM.
Hon. Organisers.

Instrument Makers and Machine
Operators must be prepared to work on
shifts—first shift commencing 7 a.m.,
second shift finishing 9.30 p.m.
Applications in writing stating age,
complete details of experience to the
MANAGER—GOVERNMENT TRAIN-
ING CENTRE, SOUTHWOLD ROAD,
WATFORD, or to the nearest Employ-
ment Exchange.

Public Notice
INSTRUCTORS
INSTRUCTORS for Machine Operating,
Fitting and Sheet-Metal working
required.
Applicants should be men of good
education and appearance and able to
maintain discipline.
Experience of Aircraft work or with
modern light alloys an advantage.
Starting rate £5 10s. per week (44
hours) Annual leave and Public Holidays with pay.
Applications in writing stating age,
experience and enclosing copies of
references, to the MANAGER, GOVERN-
MENT TRAINING CENTRE, ASCOT
WORKS, LETCHWORTH, HERTS, or
to nearest Employment Exchange.

Finland Fund
BEDFORDSHIRE APPEAL
1st LIST
The following donations have been
gratefully received by Sir Malcolm
Stewart. But and further donations will
be acknowledged in this paper next week.

	£	s.	d.
Duke of Bedford	25	0	0
Lord and Lady Luke	25	0	0
F. K. Kielberg	21	0	0
United Molasses Co. Ltd., per			
F. K. Kielberg	21	0	0
Mr. Alan and Lady Patricia			
Lennox-Boyd	20	0	0
A. T. Worsbys	20	0	0
Lord Melchett	10	10	0
Hon Claud Lambton	10	0	0
The Memorial Service at			
Sutton for Lady Burgoyne			
per Rev. W. C. Roberts	10	3	0
Harry Arnold	5	0	0
Mrs. Maurice Boden	5	0	0
General Newton	5	0	0
Mrs. Shuttleworth	5	0	0
E. J. Skinner	5	0	0
Mrs. Randall	3	3	0
Rev. Walter Wragge	3	3	0
A. Argenti	2	2	0
W. T. Ellis	2	2	0
Mr. and Mrs. Grose-Hodge	2	2	0
A. J. James	2	2	0
Sir Thomas Keens	2	2	0
James Rowland	2	2	0
Mrs. C. E. Wells	2	2	0
Sir Anthony Wingfield	2	2	0
Knox Bedford	1	0	0
Privilegia	1	0	0

2nd LIST			
Bedford Girls' Modern School,			
per Miss B. A. Tonkin	23	17	10
S. H. Whitbread	20	0	0
Bedford Modern School	16	0	0
Laporte, Ltd., Luton	10	10	0
Maurice Bennett	10	0	0
Ezra M. Street	10	0	0
Hawnes School, per Miss			
Townshend	5	0	0
F. W. Braybrooks, Ltd., Potton	5	5	0
E. G. Goodman	5	5	0
Miss M. Stansfeld	5	5	0
Henry Brown	5	0	0
Miss Ethel Janes	5	0	0
Mrs. E. Malcolmson	5	0	0
Miss A. M. Styan	5	0	0
Miss K. E. Styan	5	0	0
The British Gelatine Works Ltd.	3	3	0
Hon Constance and the			
Hon Honoria Russell	3	0	0
R. H. Couzins	2	2	0
W. Philips	2	2	0
J. B. Rodger	2	2	0
Mrs. Hugh Sartoris	2	2	0
Dr. W. A. Sharpin	2	2	0
Miss A. Wells	2	2	0
J. A. Whitchurch	2	2	0

Borough of Luton,
AIR RAID PRECAUTIONS

SIREN TESTS

ON Saturday next, 13th April, 1940, two siren
tests will be conducted in the Borough of
Luton, at 11 a.m. and 2.30 p.m. respectively, and
thence on the second Saturday in every month.

The tests will be as follows:

A STEADY NOTE (raiders passed)
for 30 seconds, followed by

A WARBLING AND INTERMITTENT
NOTE (action warning) for 25
seconds, followed by

A STEADY NOTE AGAIN (raiders
passed) for 60 seconds.

DO NOT PANIC
There will be no need for alarm.

GEO. SCOTT,
Chief Constable,
Air Raid Precautions Controller.
9th April, 1940.

waistcoat and deeply modulated voice, was the perfect gentleman's gentleman: "Jeeves to the life". But Arthur was no servile flunkey: beneath his waistcoat beat the heart of a Norfolk rebel. He regaled me with stories of terrible acts of revenge visited upon cruel and abusive masters and mistresses by their servants, of which, spitting in the soup tureen was the least objectionable. Years of loyal service had left Arthur with a deeply engrained need to be "useful" and, many years later, after he had retired and considered this to be no longer the case, he opened his oven door and gassed himself. The glorious sunny weather continued and every day brought a new threat or news of yet another disaster.

Thursday 9th May Our Mullard radio set failed and was taken away for repair by Mr Snowden, the electrical engineer who had a shop in Mill Street.

More bad news on the following day when Hitler's panzer divisions invaded Holland and Belgium and Vauxhall's management announced on the Tannoy system that our Whit Monday holiday was cancelled. Mr Snowden returned our radio and that evening we sat around it to listen to the resignation speech of the discredited Prime Minister, Neville Chamberlain, and to learn that our new War leader was to be Winston Churchill.

Saturday 11th May Took my gas mask to work this morning. Cycled to Offley and Kings Walden this afternoon, the woods carpeted with bluebells. Heard "In Town Tonight" on the radio; a policeman called and warned Clarice about our blackout. Almost daily, news of further disaster, imminent threat and mounting chaos added to our anxiety, and every evening we clustered round our radio to listen with rapt attention to the latest bulletin, whilst the realisation dawned that we were living through historic and perilous times and alone we faced the mightiest military machine in the World.

The Vauxhall Griffin emblem still hovers over the main office entrance as it did in 1940. The building is now the H.Q. of Luton Chamber Business.

Tuesday 14th May In the evening we heard the mocking nasal tones of William Joyce, a henchman of the British Fascist leader, Sir Oswald Mosley, broadcasting from the Nazi "New British Broadcasting Station", and on the following evening we heard of the Dutch surrender, overwhelmed by the might of Hitler's "blitzkrieg".

Thursday 16th May Saw "The Hunchback of Notre Dame" at the Palace cinema tonight, and later we listened to President Roosevelt's speech; weather very sunny all day.

Saturday 18th May Ivor and I saw "Gulliver's Travels" and "The Five Little Peppers" at the Savoy cinema this afternoon and listened to "Itma" tonight – hot and sunny all day.

Sunday 19th May Our family gathered round our radio set tonight to listen to the heartening defiance of our new Prime Minister. Churchill spared us nothing and spoke frankly of our desperate situation, "behind our army stands a group of shattered States and bludgeoned races....upon all of whom the long night of barbarism will descend......unless we conquer, as conquer we must, as conquer we shall."

Dad and Bill Creighton had no illusions about Churchill: he was a

The oak panelled interior of the main office "well" was normally filled with busy typists, the staircase on the left led to the Cost office, the one on the right led to a deeply carpeted corridor, the office of Managing Director, Charles Bartlett, the offices of senior executives and the Company's Board room.

A busy wartime scene at the Canteen Gate with a sandbagged air raid refuge for the gatekeeper in the foreground, P Block on the left, and a V.M. plant dustcart parked on the roadside. The canteen's loading dock for supplies is on the right and the tree beyond the line of trucks stood by the plant's fire station: the distant houses are on the Vauxhall estate near the airport.

leader of the hated Tories with a long history of brutality towards the working class, but they detested fascism even more; they warmed to his fighting stance and contrasted it with the contemptible Chamberlain and his colleagues, the appeasers of Hitler whom everyone blamed for the present peril and the rout of our army now engaged in a desperate fighting retreat to the French coast.

Monday 20th May Mum and Ivor took the bus to Letchworth and visited our former home. Evening classes commenced and for the first time I walked down the hill to the Technical College on Park Square for two hours of mechanical drawing. The following night it was mathematics and National Identity Cards were issued, to be carried at all times, reflecting a growing public unease about a treacherous "fifth column", a factor we were assured in the Nazi Blitzkrieg and the conquest of France and the Low Countries, as it had been in Spain where the term was first coined.

Thursday 23rd May "My shoes went to the cobblers". Eating a fish and chip supper tonight and gathered round our radio, we heard that the German army had reached the Channel coast at Boulogne.

Friday 24th May Tomorrow was Norton Road School's annual Mayday celebration when the juniors dance around the beribboned maypoles, the senior boys longsword team would demonstrate their skills, and a scratch orchestra led by Mr Poppy and his violin would play traditional airs as the lovely June Higgs was enthroned under a bower of lilac and May blossom. Mayday festivities in Letchworth were rooted in the William Morris style of English socialism, which nurtured the native folk culture of a pre-industrial age and permeated the first Garden City since the founding days and which, in its first pioneer school, was a particularly strong tradition. The day was a major event in the school's calendar, with busy preparations in the months before and the senior's election of a May Queen from the girls in the upper forms: it was also a great day for reunions, when old pupils greeted their veteran teachers to recount the school's pioneering days and mingle with the happy throng of children and parents. For two weeks or more I had lived in eager anticipation of Mayday and the chance to renew acquaintance with my erstwhile classmates and one classmate in particular, June Higgs, for whom I nursed an undeclared love; but today my hopes were dashed when the Tannoy loudspeakers broadcast a management announcement that in the coming weekend the plant would work as normal in view of the urgent need to replace the huge losses of trucks captured or destroyed in France.

That evening the uninspiring King George addressed the nation on

This view of the plant taken about 1950 shows Y Block situated between the main railway line to London and Gipsy Lane and the long vanished LNER line to Welwyn, in the background the new AA Block built on the site of Luton's old sewage works.

the radio, the weather turned to rain and I prepared to spend the weekend at work sunk in the deepest gloom.

Saturday 25th May Worked all day, mooning about the office under the watchful eye of Mr Morris and envying brother Ivor who was enjoying the Mayday celebrations. Walked into town after work to buy drawing instruments and listened to "In Town Tonight" on our radio.

The routine of evening classes at the "Tech" on Park Square got into its full stride in the following week, mechanical drawing on Monday, maths on Tuesday and English on Thursday.

Tuesday 4th June 1940.

The staff of Vauxhall's Planning records office photographed by draughtsman John Wright on the sports ground in front of X Block.

Those I recall are:
Front row left to right: Phylis Cook, Joyce Gurney, Bert Waller, Norman Morris, Arthur Fulcher, ——? Far right Lulu Warters.
2nd row: Renee Shreaves, Florrie Brooker, Doris Randall, Owen Hardisty (behind Norman Morris).
3rd row: Peter Griggs, Mick Whiteley, ——?, ——?. Vick White, ——?.
Back row: Trevor Runneckles, Frank Collins.

Wednesday 29th May The Tannoy announced that work would continue again through the coming weekend. Dad cleaned out the rainwater tank over our outside lavatory.

Friday 31st May It was announced that the British Expeditionary Force was leaving Northern France. The first works identity passes were issued in the form of a crude symbol stamped on our wage packets, whose colour and design would change weekly and which had to be produced on demand at the gates.

Saturday 1st June Our local air raid Warden's post was hidden behind a high wall of sandbags at St Anne's Church in Crawley Green Road, and it was there that we joined an anxious crowd in the evening to have our gas masks modified by the attachment of a vivid green filter bound to the snout with adhesive tape; this, we were assured by an elderly warden, would protect us from the latest deadly gas devised by Hitler's chemists: then it was home to listen to the familiar "In Town Tonight" on our radio. The first week in June and the weather was glorious with the sun shining from a cloudless sky.

Tuesday 4th June My diary notes that the evacuation of our shattered army was almost complete and at lunchtime on that day the entire Planning Records staff was requested by Mr Morris to assemble on the sports ground in front of X Block for a photograph. The photographer was John Wright, a jig and tool draughtsman, and whether it was his idea or that of Norman Morris to record us for posterity I never knew, but there we are, sitting crosslegged on the grass or on the rockery behind. Mr Morris, as befitted his position, sat in the centre with arms folded; flanked by his deputy clerk, Bert Waller, and Arthur Fulcher, with his splendid polished boots to the fore, and Miss Randall, the chief typist, with eight other female secretaries and typists and seven of us office boys perched on the embankment and grinning cheekily at the camera.

Wednesday 5th June Heard that we were to have next Sunday off. Mum bought cases for our Identity cards.

Thursday 6th June Beautiful weather continues. My wage packet contained the vast sum of twenty three shillings, boosted by overtime pay for that miserable Whitsun weekend, and my diary noted ominously "the Germans have attacked the Somme".

CHAPTER FOUR

Dunkirk – digging in

June–July 1940

Workers and bosses   Hot weather, Horlicks and lime juice
The army invades Vauxhall – the Nazis invade Paris
Feverish preparations – constant ARP drills
The big dig – our shelter arrives
Machine guns on the spoil heaps – sentries on the gates
Hitler raves and threatens

After two months of running errands and delivering mail around the plant, its lay-out, the various areas and their managers were becoming familiar to me. Area Managers were feared by the workforce: not because they were particularly callous or lacking in humanity, but because of the power they had to dismiss workers. It is difficult to understand in later years the terrors that "getting the sack" held for those who had lived through years of the great depression; minor misdemeanours such as smoking in the lavatories were punished by one or two days suspension, but more serious crimes, theft of company property, "clocking in" absent workmates or fighting, merited instant dismissal. In rare cases when a "jackets off" dispute became too heated, the issue was usually resolved by fisticuffs on the patch of rank grass adjoining the sewerage works, but on one occasion violence erupted in the canteen at lunch time when a diner had a plateful of rice pudding smashed on his head and the sight of the stunned victim, rice pudding and blood streaming down his face, remained long in my memory.

Frank Ash was Area Manager in "lower 17 division" where engine parts were machined and engines built and tested; his son David was an apprentice in the school in P Block and soon to receive shrapnel wounds in his head when a bomb burst in Kimpton Road. George Barker's domain was the back axle area in Blocks P and Q and Charlie Snoxell was manager in the gearshop where he occupied an office situated like Frank Ash's eyrie on a high platform, so that the machining lines and the production operatives were in his full view. Charlie's deputy and General Foreman was Jack Norwood, an eccentric and well respected character whose unruly hair and buckteeth earned him the nickname "Trotsky" but whose competence as an engineer was conceded by everyone – even Dad.

The Manager of the truck assembly line and the rectification department in K Block was Bob Whitworth, whose beautiful sixteen year old daughter Marjorie was soon to join the typists in our office and embark on a sly romance with Harold Blunn, a handsome young toolroom apprentice, much to the delight of Arthur Fulcher and the frowning disapproval of Mr Morris.

Sunday 9th June My first day off in three weeks, cycled to Letchworth to spend the day at the swimming pool with Russell and Jack; Mrs Rogers insisted that I have dinner with them before cycling back to Luton.

Monday 10th June Italy declared war on us today – President Roosevelt spoke tonight.

A task I regarded as very strange was added to my duties when Mr Morris instructed me to obtain two white enamelled pails with lids from the Tool bond stores together with two large tin mugs, a piece of clean timber from the pattern shop foreman, a large tin of Horlicks, (a malted milk bedtime drink) and two bottles of Roses concentrated lime juice from the canteen shop.

I was instructed to empty two mugfuls of Horlicks and one bottle of lime juice into each bucket, top up with water at the washroom tap, stir with the stick and place one bucket in the Die Design drawing office and the other in the Jig and Tool drawing office: apparently this "perk" of free refreshment was a long standing custom in hot weather and although the brew with its floating scum of Horlicks looked revolting, its taste was quite pleasant.

Wednesday 12th June Soldiers of a regular army unit were today stationed at the plant; they took over the peacetime car showrooms opposite the main offices as a barracks and immediately started to dig entrenchments and sand bagged gun emplacements in the spoil heaps which overlooked V and X Blocks on St Anne's Hill. Morning roll calls and drill were held on the sports field in front of our block and shouted commands could be heard through the open windows of the offices as the staff sought relief from the sweltering heat.

Whether it was the long hours of work, the heat or the growing apprehension of what might happen, normally placid people were inclined to instant irritable reactions. Mr Morris was reputed to be a lay preacher and certainly his deep bass voice could thunder out over the office hubbub when he chose to.

Given some perceived reason for annoyance, his bellowed command "Fulcher" sent Arthur scurrying to answer the summons; after a few minutes he returned to his post by the filing cabinets, furious that the unspoken contract between master and servant had been broken – respect in return for loyal service.

Lapsing into his ancestral Norfolk dialect, and with undiminished fury, Arthur confided in me "that guvnor of ours do hev a voice like an elephant farting down a drain" and left me helpless with suppressed laughter.

Thursday 13th June Sister Clarice got a job at Vauxhall working in W Block Parts department office.

Friday 14th June The Germans have entered Paris. Saw "Tower of London" at the Odeon tonight.

Monday 17th June Went to evening class tonight; mother made out our new ration books. France surrendered to the Nazis. "People are very anxious".

Tuesday 18th June The two machine gun posts in the spoil heaps are now completed and manned by soldiers – Bren gun muzzles and steel helmets glimpsed between the parapet and sandbagged roof.

After evening class the family listened in silence to Churchill's speech on the radio; he warned of the coming battle in the air, the imminent invasion and the danger of seeking to indict those responsible for the present catastrophe – "there are too many in it". He ended with a rallying call to arms and an expression of confidence in the people.

On my frequent visits to their secretary's office to clear the "out" trays, I glimpsed a frowning Mr Johnson and his deputy through a mist of tobacco smoke, with planners and engineers gathered round and a welter of drawings and specifications spread over desks and tables.

Phones rang, typewriters clattered; there were trains to be caught, hotels to be booked and I was sent pedalling furiously to the wages office to encash cheques for expenses; the atmosphere of urgency and anxiety was palpable and hung over our office like a cloud.

Everyone sensed the impending danger and feverish preparations were under way to meet the expected onslaught; concrete pillboxes were constructed and trenches dug at strategic points and neighbourhood air raid wardens reacted instantly to the slightest infringement of the blackout. Brother Ivor and myself attended the frequent fire fighting demonstrations on the open ground near the St Anne's ARP post and learned to crawl on our bellies towards the blazing magnesium with sandbag and stirrup pump nozzle, whilst a large reservoir to hold water was being built with great haste on Powdrill's field between Devon Road and Vauxhall's boundary fence, the excavating machines working late into the evening.

Thursday 20th June Luton Council delivered our Anderson air raid shelter; sections of heavy gauge corrugated steel arches to be bolted together and erected in a pit at the bottom of our garden.

Saturday 22nd June The digging commenced, with gangs of navvies hacking at the heavy clay to sink our shelter and those of our neighbours – the Hardys, the Bougheys and the Creightons, but so hard was the

With slicked down hair and wearing my Burton's suit. A portrait from the studio of William Harold Cox of 29 Wellington Street. In 1940 the teenager had still to be invented: childhood left behind us at fourteen, we became replicas of our parents and elders; teenage fashion, music and lifestyle were in the unimagined future.

ground that the diggers often worked late into the evening and it was more than a week before the task was completed. With the steelwork erected in the pit, the next task was to cover the arched roof with sufficient earth to give some protection and screen the gaping entrance against blast and splinters.

Dad and I spent every spare moment heaving nodules of red clay and flint onto the shelter roof, and a week later we constructed a blast wall of earth filled boxes and sandbags to shield the entrance.

Sunday 23rd June The French leaders signed the armistice with Hitler.

Monday 24th June Sister Clarice started work in her new job in Vauxhall's Parts department in W Block. At 1 a m during that night the wailing sirens woke us and it was 3 hours before the "all clear" marked the end of an uneventful "alert". The spine chilling experience of the undulating siren in the dead of night, however, must have aroused fear in others, besides myself, for the following evening a party of neighbours came knocking on our door collecting money for the purchase of stirrup pumps.

Thursday 27th June We heard that the coming Sunday was to be a rest day. After work I cycled into town and after long deliberation bought a pair of binoculars at Alder's pawnshop in Bute Street. If the Nazi bombers came, I was determined to see them first.

Sunday 30th June In glorious sunshine I cycled through the villages of Willian and Weston and spent a lazy afternoon with my erstwhile school friends on the Radwell water meadows. Arriving home at 7.30 I found the air raid shelter complete but still lacking a decent covering of earth.

Monday 1st July Made a wall of earth filled boxes and sandbags in front of the shelter entrance.

Sunday 7th July Ivor and I cycled to St Albans and viewed the cathedral, the Roman ruins of Verulamium and the old Round House pub by the lake.

My father, Bill Hardisty, photographed by a colleague with blueprints under his arm in Vauxhall's X Block toolroom: because of clothes rationing he made use of my long-dead grandfather's carpenter's apron with its large front pocket, handy for tools and drawings.

Tuesday 9th July Ivor lost his gas mask at school but found it later.

Friday 12th July This morning, armed sentries stood at every gate and entrance door to the plant with orders to search everyone. At St Anne's gate, fresh faced and embarrassed young soldiers rummaged through lunch boxes and women's handbags, scrutinising identity cards and works passes under the watchful eyes of their N.C.O.s.

Saturday 13th July The office staff worked until noon and I spent the afternoon shovelling yet more earth onto the Anderson's roof, a surprisingly difficult and exhausting job as the heavy lumps of clay and flint tended to roll back down the curved roof to ground level. In the evening I saw "Arouse and Beware" at the Savoy cinema and afterwards walked slowly home up Crawley Green Road and Rutland Path in the afterglow of a fine summer day.

Sunday 14th July Cycled up Kimpton Road to Bendish and Whitwell this afternoon. Old Mrs Evans, our neighbour in Green Lane, Letchworth, who had since moved to Richmond Hill in Luton, visited us in the evening.

Evening class exams were held in the following week.

Thursday 18th July The final class of the term.

Friday 19th July Yet another hot, sunny day and Hitler finally lost his patience with us; after work I strolled along Windmill Road, across Manor Road "Rec" and into Park Street where I had my haircut at Charlie Inglis's barbers shop. My diary records "there was an important meeting in the Reichstag tonight" and that we listened to the wireless when the BBC evening News bulletin carried the sound of Hitler's voice bellowing threats of our impending annihilation and promising a "final" attack on England if we did not see sense.

CHAPTER FIVE

The onslaught begins

July–September 1940

Hotter and still hotter

Radio talks and films to boost morale

"Altogether – light your bricks" fiasco

"Haw Haw" taunts us – red sky over London.

Blitzkreig hits Vauxhall – Dennis killed

Unexpected holiday – aftermath and narrow escapes

The army leaves Vauxhall   Evening classes commence

Saturday 20th July The weather settled into a pattern of heat and humidity, sunshine and thundery showers; ventured into town tonight to see a morale boosting film "We Are Not Alone" at the Savoy Cinema.

Sunday 21st July Yet another demonstration of fire fighting on the usual patch of grass near the St Anne's Warden's post; I wondered if the stirrup pump was purchased from the proceeds of the door to door collection.

Monday, Tuesday and all the following week the oppressive heat continued, with the sweating draughtsmen working at their boards by the open blackout shutters, whilst I replenished the buckets of lime juice and Horlicks at regular intervals and the distant shouted commands of the army unit N.CO.s reached us on the breathless air, and every evening found me, shovel in hand, throwing more earth onto our shelter: we and all our neighbours had taken Churchill's warning seriously and now seemed obsessed with the desire to burrow deeper into the earth like human moles.

Friday 26th July The evening BBC News bulletin claimed 28 enemy planes were shot down yesterday – I scanned the evening skies with my binoculars but saw nothing.

Sunday 28th July A rest day. I pushed my bike up the steep Spittlesea Lane, past the grim red brick façade of the isolation hospital, and loitered by the airport boundary fence watching the trainee pilots endlessly practising circuits and landings in their little yellow mono planes and lazily taxiing on the airport's grass.

Thursday 1st August A rumour circulated in the office yesterday that holidays were to be allowed but quickly denied today. This evening Ivor and I walked up the footpath which climbs through the allotments and air raid shelters at the rear of Vauxhall's press shops and walked on past the airport fence to the romantic ruin of Someries Castle.

Friday 2nd August Holidays were re-instated and I was allocated three days by Mr Morris.

Everyone yearned for respite from work and the heat. Workshops and offices sweltered under the camouflage screens; the construction gangs labouring to complete Y Block worked stripped of shirts, and the distant Someries wood and Spittlesea hospital shimmered and danced in the noonday heat haze. Meantime the showers and humidity had given way to hot "harvesting" weather, forever associated in my mind with the summer of 1940, whilst Vauxhall's workers, Luton's citizens and the whole of England waited for the onslaught which must surely come, held in suspense by the reports of increasing attacks all along the South Coast.

Sunday 4th August A beautiful warm day. I boarded the Letchworth bus with mother who was intent on meeting her old friends and neighbours and exchanging all the gossip and news. I sought out my friends Russell and Jack and spent the afternoon with them at the open air swimming pool on Norton Common, teasing the girls and soaking up the sun on the terrace. Russell and I had tea with his parents at their cottage in Church Lane and afterwards joined the customary Sunday crowds on the Common, where we met our old form teacher Mr Youngman, before catching the evening bus to Luton.

Saturday 10th August Luton's air raid sirens were tested in the morning and again in the afternoon, their hideous wailing adding to the atmosphere of apprehension and foreboding. About midday Clarice's friend, Grace Northwood, and her husband, Owen, arrived from Letchworth to have tea with us. Owen wearing his "hospital blue" uniform still traumatised and recovering from his wounds received in the French debacle.

Sunday 11th August The following day the weather changed briefly to cold and cloudy and the BBC news reported fifty German planes shot down; that evening we listened to the Bradford author, J B Priestley, giving one of his fireside chats: his delivery was slow and reassuring as he mocked Hitler and the Nazis in his flat Yorkshire dialect and probably did more to "stiffen the sinews" than even Churchill's defiant oratory.

As the Nazi attacks increased in scale and ferocity, anti-Nazi films and morale-boosting radio programmes became our spiritual food, our "Dutch courage" to brace us for the ordeal ahead, and this week was no exception.

Monday 12th August I saw "Pastor Hall" at the Union Cinema, a film about a heroic German clergyman defying Hitler, and on Wednesday a

BBC offering "The Land we Defend" followed by "Armies of Free Men" on Friday: all designed to arouse patriotic fervour and put us in good heart.

My diary entry for Friday also records that 169 German planes were claimed shot down yesterday, that I skipped breakfast as I was feeling unwell and in the evening I walked the length of Powdrill's field to inspect progress on the emergency reservoir where excavators were throwing up great banks of earth.

Saturday 17th August There were no German air raids on Britain today, the day was hot and sunny and brother Ivor and I spent a pleasant afternoon at the Bath Road swimming pool. I also noted that Council workers delivered "smoke bricks" to our house and every house in Luton on the previous evening. These were made of wood shavings and bitumen and when smouldering gave off dense clouds of smoke: the idea was that when we all ignited them in our living room grates at a given time, the resulting smoke would screen Luton and its factories from the bombers.

Sunday 18th August Weather very sunny this morning, dull with rain later. Lethargic due to headache; "many German aircraft were shot down today".

Monday 19th August Headache persists – took Genaspirin. 142 German planes claimed yesterday.

This evening was trial time for Luton's smoke screen and at 8 o'clock thousands of households dutifully lit their smoke bricks and a host of domestic chimneys belched dirty smoke. The evening was dull and a light rain was falling as the smoke drifted slowly over houses and gardens: from the vantage point of Rutland Path I watched the effect in the valley below as the crowded terraces of Park Town and New Town all contributed their quota to the general murk: the overall result was a smelly, foggy atmosphere, but Luton was in no way hidden.

Tuesday 20th August Mr Churchill made a speech today. Once again
everyone was instructed to light their smoke bricks at 8 o'clock: by now,
however, thick soot deposits which had built up from the previous
night's exercise caught fire, resulting in several spectacular chimney
fires, with the screening effect no better than the night before. The
general consensus amongst our neighbours was that the whole crazy
scheme was a dismal flop: a conclusion doubtless shared by the
authorities as it was never tried again.

Wednesday 21st August A "yellow" warning before noon.

Thursday 22nd August Got extra pay for the Whitsun and August
Bank holidays. Watched yet another incendiary bomb demonstration
outside Powdrill's this evening and then cycled to Cockernhoe.

Friday 23rd August Four Italian warships were sunk today.

Saturday 24th August Bought shoes from the Co-op in Manchester
Street. The air raid sirens sounded at five to four.

Sunday 25th August The whole family walked down to the Vauxhall
canteen this evening for a concert by the orchestra under the baton of
Mr Fred Green. After arriving home we were warned by an air raid
warden that we were showing a light.

Tuesday 27th August Dad is enjoying his allocated three day holiday
break. Cycled up the Bedford Road towards Streatley in the evening and
later we listened to the broadcast of the British Fascist, William Joyce,
whose ridiculous nasal upper class English drawl had earned him the
nickname "Lord Haw Haw", mimicked by every would-be comedian

but whose claims were only believed by the gullible.

There was an air raid warning during the night but we slept through it.

Wednesday 28th August A fine sunny day and mother, Dad and brother Ivor went by Green Line bus to St Albans in the afternoon. In the evening we listened to "Lord Haw Haw" on our radio and stayed up late to see the distant flashes and red glow of a raid on London, our first experience of an event which was to become only too common in the coming months.

Thursday 29th August Dad spent the last of his brief holiday by taking the train to London, probably driven by curiosity to see the results of last night's bombing. Once again, in the evening we listened to "Lord Haw Haw"'s threats and taunts.

Friday 30th August was warm and the sun shone from a cloudless sky as it had done for the past week. One of my duties was to collect all the outgoing mail from the Planning Department's suite of offices and deliver it to the mailing department boy who would then take it to his sorting point next to the commissionaire's office in the entrance to V Block. Mr Johnson and his deputy Mr Thursby smoked constantly, the air in their offices heavy with the scent of pipe tobacco, but for ordinary mortals the factory rules forbade smoking in office or workshop and the only refuge for the smoker was in the privacy of a lavatory cubicle, where a few minutes deep inhalation dispelled cares and restored calm to jangled nerves. So it was that at half past four I handed over our mail to Dennis Orchard, and with Woodbines and matches in my pocket headed for the cloakroom, where I chatted to John Wright the draughtsman who had photographed us some weeks before; we both leaned on the wall whilst waiting for a vacant toilet and gazing at a small patch of sky visible through a partly open blackout shutter.

This photograph was taken minutes after the air raid of the 30th August with a huge column of smoke rising from burning oil drums and vehicles. V Block water tower can be seen at the base of the column, St. Annes estate on the left horizon and Luton airport on the right.

Some five minutes later we heard distant thunder which we later discovered was the sound of the first bombs bursting on the airport. This puzzled us at the time as the sky was cloudless, but within a few seconds the noise rose to a deafening crescendo and the building shook violently as the toilet doors were flung open and the occupants, frantically fastening braces and belts, fled for cover.

John Wright and I rushed out, dived for the office floor and crawled under a large wooden coat hanger stand where we instinctively covered our heads with our hands for protection against the glass and debris

Bombs cratered the sports ground in front of X Block; the groundsman's abandoned diesel roller and the screens, both riddled with shrapnel, stand forlornly on the cricket pitch, whilst K Block and the burned out rectification shop can be seen on the far side of the ground. The sports field was used as a daily parade ground by a regular army unit stationed at the plant between June and September 1940.

showering down, and lay with eyes screwed tight and breathing suspended.

When finally the noise abated, we discovered that we could not stand up and realised that the big steam heating pipes in the roof had fallen, broken the coat stand and pinned us to the floor; within minutes however, our workmates freed us unhurt, but soaked with filthy water from the broken pipes.

Scrambling to our feet we sprinted for the shelters; down the stairway at the end of the block we joined toolmakers and die makers in overalls, managers and draughtsmen in smart suits and typists in summer frocks; even Mr Morris, dignity forgotten, fled with the rest.

Emerging into the daylight, the rectification block facing us across the sports ground was ablaze from end to end and the huge stockpile of oil drums by the end of V Block was spouting red flame and thrusting a huge column of black smoke into the sky.

Under the camouflage netting which spanned the road we ran, when the rattle of machine guns was heard overhead and everyone dropped face down in the cinders bordering the road; we were assured later that the firing was not aimed at us but was the gunfire of a Spitfire pursuing one of the Heinkels which it shot down near Kimpton.

The mangled remains of a MW truck on the road leading to V and X Blocks is examined by a steel helmeted worker, probably a member of Vauxhall's Home Guard Company.

The bomb shelters for the staff in V and X Blocks were underground concrete lined tunnels with rudimentary wooden seating, situated on land at the airport side of X Block near the skid test pan, and to reach safety involved a run of two or three hundred yards; towards them we sprinted, down the ramp, round the entrance blast wall, to collapse shaking and shocked on the wooden seats. I was aware of wet cloth clinging to my trembling legs and noticed for the first time my smart

V Block, otherwise known as the experimental Block, housed the engineering drawing office, engine test chambers, experimental rigs and the facilities needed for the production of prototypes: it was here that the components for Britain's first twelve Whittle jet engines were produced. Its landmark water tower with its camouflaged walls and painted false windows was intended to deceive the bombers; the shrapnel pitted brickwork however is evidence that it failed.

grey trousers, bought by mother a month before, now drenched in filthy water and cinders.

Soon talk became animated, euphoria and relief that we had survived spread through the shelter, and when some minutes later we heard the town's sirens finally sounding the "alert" it was greeted with ironic cheers and Anglo Saxon obscenities.

Shocked though we were, there were still moments of humour; a sales

A bomb which narrowly missed the Gear shop and the Metallurgical Laboratory blasted out a wall in the Heat Treatment shop in B Block exposing the carbonising furnaces.

representative from a Sheffield cutting tool firm sat opposite me, resplendent in a smart double-breasted suit; he had been in the die shop when he had been deluged with copious quantities of soot and grime dislodged by the blast from the roof girders, and he now sat wearily, with blackened face and a thick layer of soot on his brilliantined hair, pretending not to hear snide remarks about Al Jolson.

After ten minutes or so, curiosity overcame caution, and, as everything was quiet apart from the sound of exploding oil drums, we ventured out to see the still smouldering ruin of the rectification block and the burning oil dump, and it was only then that I noticed the line of huge craters pitting the sports ground.

A bomb crater near the oil storage dump; the side of Q Block with its screens of camouflage netting can be seen top right.

The scene of devastation viewed from the end of V Block with Q Block on the right and Someries Wood and Spitalsea Isolation Hospital on the horizon beyond K Block.

A fellow office boy and I decided, after hesitating for half an hour to view the damage, to make our way to the "bombproof" K Block surgery, a windowless concrete blockhouse built in the pre-war crisis years, where first aid was being given to a long line of injured people lying on stretchers in the roadway; then past burnt out cars and up the slope to V Block, its pitted walls, shattered windows and the gaping hole where the entrance, the stairway and the mailing office sorting point had been and where Dennis, the commissionaire, and five others had died.

By this time, feeling tired and hungry, I made for St Anne's Hill and the comforts of home, but found the gate closed and an armed sentry

Blast and shrapnel damaged V Block experimental engineering workshop and the pattern shop on the ground floor and the engineering drawing office on the floor above.

there who explained that he had orders to let no-one through as there were many unexploded bombs in the ground nearby. Working my way along the boundary fence, I met my father and a neighbour, Alf Hill, both of whom worked in the tool room, Alf's son Ivan and our neighbour Bill Creighton, who were all anxious to get home and re-assure their families. Frustrated and angry, we soon discovered that if we seized the bottom of the chain link fencing and all heaved together, it was possible to wriggle on our bellies underneath the wire and escape to the narrow strip of rough grassland between the works fence and Devon Road.

Devon Road, Rutland Crescent and the whole of St Anne's estate was strangely quiet, and arriving home we were mystified to find our house and all the neighbouring houses unlocked and deserted, and it was a long two hours before mother, sister Clarice and Bessy Creighton returned to explain that they had been directed to St Anne's Church Rest Centre because of the many unexploded bombs nearby which were suspected of having delayed action fuses; in the event, none did explode and, for many weeks following, the army bomb disposal teams toiled to dig them out.

After a meal and several cups of tea to calm our jangled nerves, Dad, brother Ivor and I walked down Rutland Path and Crawley Green Hill in the warm evening sunlight to inspect the ruined Corporation Bus

The morning after; steel helmets worn in case of falling debris, workers sweep the littered floor in K Block.

garage in Park Street, with its gaping roof, wrecked buses and the bombed terraced houses in the surrounding streets strewn with rubble and broken furniture.

Saturday 31st August I wrote to my schoolfriends Jack Taylor and Russell Rogers to assure them we were safe. An air raid "alert" sounded, with the "all clear" 15 minutes later.

Sunday 1st September Cycled to Kings Walden this afternoon and saw some deer in the park. Saw notice about work posted outside the factory tonight "the delayed action bombs have not yet exploded."

Building workers survey wrecked offices in V Block: Note the shrapnel pitted walls.

Damaged OY trucks amongst the devastation of K Block; trucks were rolling off the assembly line once more when production resumed after a few days.

The gaping entrance to V Block where a bomb exploded in the stairwell, killing the commissionaire, the mailing department office boy, Dennis Orchard, and five others.

Monday 2nd September Cycled through Harpenden to St Albans in glorious sunny weather this morning, parked my bike against the town's medieval clock tower, paid my sixpence and climbed the stairs to gaze upon the curfew bell and enjoy the view over the ancient city. Saw "Nell Gwynne" at the Alma cinema tonight and had a chip supper.

Tuesday 3rd September the first anniversary of the war. Another air raid warning blared out this morning and my unexpected holiday ended when I reluctantly returned to work at midday and received a severe reprimand from Mr Morris for being three hours late.

Wednesday 4th September X Block was strangely silent today, no muffled roar of machinery or the clang of steel on steel sounded through our office partition wall; on the pretext of an internal mail delivery, I stepped cautiously into the die shop, where I found the main bays evacuated and clusters of plant engineers standing under the flanking balconies staring intently upwards.

Their concern, I was told, was whether the bombs had fractured or distorted the building's steel frame and made unsafe the heavy lifting cranes which travelled on overhead rails.

There was no time to carry out a slow, detailed inspection of the structure, so now the crane's drivers, suspended in their cabs forty or fifty feet above us, tweaked the controls and slowly drove the whole length of the bays and back again without incident; anxiety was dispelled and, with an almost audible sigh of relief, the cranes were pronounced fit to resume lifting heavy dies and tank turret castings.

Emergency squads of builders and labourers were busy all over the plant, the tons of shattered glass swept up and replaced by window panes of sheet steel produced in the press shop, and army trucks were once more rolling off the K Block assembly line after a break of only three days.

My own job resumed its now familiar routine of filing forms,

Kimpton Road and the front of P Block after a bomb burst in the roadway, spraying the Apprentice School and offices with shrapnel. Note the elaborately painted camouflage. (Compare with the 1990 view).

delivering mail and helping Arthur issue blueprints and, of course, hauling heavy loads of paper to be lashed with thick parcel twine to the carrier of my works' bike. Struggling up the slope towards V Block I remembered my schoolboy innocence of a mere twelve months ago when air raids and bombs were a hidden mystery, but now I became for the first time aware of the awesome power of high explosives: bomb fragments had smashed huge holes in the concrete wall and steel girders were penetrated like cardboard: the groundsman's diesel roller, now riddled with holes, stood forlornly on the cricket pitch and the devastated V Block frontage gaped at the burnt out vehicles and craters. Dennis and the others who perished there stood no chance in the face of such violence.

Before demolition began, a view of Kimpton Road and P Block taken in January 1990. Bomb damage and camouflage paint long gone, the frontage is basically unchanged in half a century.

A private of Vauxhall's Home Guard Company clad in denim overalls, work boots and steel helmet, stood with his rifle in the "stand easy" position by a roped off area on the corner of Q Block guarding nothing in particular, while the smell of pulverised brick and cement hung heavy in the air.

My mail delivery to the K Block office took me past the rectification shop, where steel helmeted gangs were towing out wrecked trucks and tangled roof members and where I discovered that many of the clusters of bombs which had destroyed the shop had landed in the filter beds of Luton's sewage treatment works situated alongside Eaton Green Road and K Block, the resulting explosions plastering the walls with a noxious crust of raw sewage and clinker which stank to high heaven and

A sergeant and two privates of an army bomb disposal squad plant their boots on a recovered bomb.

gave the brickwork a more effective camouflage coating than the paint.

Everywhere people were talking about their experiences on Friday afternoon and accounts of amazing escapes were circulating; a 500 kg bomb which fortunately failed to explode penetrated the roof and two concrete floors in P Block to end up in the basement machine shop with a split casing, whereupon the machinists fled their workplace in record time. Amongst the heat treatment furnaces in Q Block, a bomb burst on a roof girder, injuring George Wright, one of the operatives; although George's legs were peppered with shrapnel, he carried a wounded workmate on his back to K Block surgery, only to be told that he was dead.

Thursday 5th September Heard that 194 bombs fell on Friday. Listened to "Lord Haw Haw" tonight.

Friday 6th September Mr Morris ordered me to take our departmental bike to the New Hudson Cycle Company (Partridge's) in Chapel Street for repair, and after work I walked down to Charlie Inglis's barber shop in Park Street for a haircut. King Carol of Rumania abdicated. The warm sunny weather continues.

Bomb squad soldiers with Frank Southwell, Vauxhall's ARP Controller and a Nazi bomb, one of many dug out of the spoil heaps at the rear of X and V Blocks after the raid of 30th August. In postwar years this area was landscaped to create a memorial garden to Vauxhall's war dead, but it was latter flattened and became a car park for finished vehicles.

Saturday 7th September Visited Wardown Museum and afterwards
swam and sunbathed at the Bath Road open air pool. Ivor cycled to
Clothall to gather blackberries. That evening the sky beyond East Hyde
and Harpenden glowed a vivid red as the London Docks burned, and
twice during the night Luton's sirens blared out.

Sunday 8th September Nightly alarms continue – there were a total
of five last night and so far one tonight. We fixed up a single bed
mattress for extra comfort in our shelter.

Vauxhall's ARP Controller Frank Southwell and a soldier of the Army Bomb Disposal team
examine two "duds" recovered from the sports ground and made safe. Q Block and the
camouflage screen can be seen in the background.

Vauxhall's car showroom built in the 1930s; it was used briefly as a barracks in the summer of 1940 by a regular army unit stationed at the plant and later by Vauxhall's Home Guard company: its flat roof mounted the factory's only anti-aircraft defence, twin Lewis guns which were manned during "alerts" but never fired in anger. Pictured in 1990 before demolition of the canteen and many of the older buildings.

Tuesday 10th September The Luton Corporation men called today to inform us that our shelter is not deep enough but offered no solution. "London is still being bombed". Enquired about a rest period at work; two alarms during the night.

  In the warm, still evenings of that early Autumn, I often sought peace and the illusion of safety by cycling along the Lilley Bottom Lane in the dusk towards Kings Walden and Whitwell, with the wood pigeons murmuring in the roadside elms and the harvest still stacked in fields of stubble. The turmoil of the factory and the bombing seemed like a distant dream, until the faint wailing of the sirens signalled another long night of cramped discomfort in our garden refuge. At some point during this time the factory's regular army unit was quietly withdrawn for more important duties, and the daily gateway inspection of our works' passes was left to Sergeant Simpson's squad of commissionaires, armed only with polished boots and an intimidating manner.

Wednesday 11th September Air raid warning at ten minutes past noon and two alarms already tonight; heard the Prime Minister speak on the radio tonight, warning us of the imminent invasion and urging everyone to prepare to do their duty "whatever it may be". He compared the coming week with the historical threat from the Spanish Armada or Napoleon's Army poised at Boulogne.

Thursday 12th September Weather dull and raining, awoke late and ran to get to work on time. Mr Morris informed me that my rest period would start tomorrow. Did some lettering for the Tool Inspection clerk, Bob Dale, and earned myself sixpence. Joined the hundreds of boys and girls enrolling for evening classes at the Technical College in Park Square tonight.

Friday 13th September Slept until noon: several air raid alarms last night and three tonight. Went into town with mother this afternoon and ordered a suit at Burton's. Weather, dull, heavy rain.

Saturday, 14th September Spent the morning in bed trying to compensate for the hours of sleep lost in the past two weeks; there was an air raid alarm this afternoon and two have already sounded tonight.

CHAPTER SIX

Alarms by night and day

September–November 1940

Park Street's monster land mine

A new hobby – collecting shrapnel

Percival's in peril – landmine snagged in their roof

Spy plane takes our photo   Fling more clay on the shelter

Stooging around – the airport's useless planes

Cold nights and misery – escape sought in reading

Slaughter in Old Bedford Road

Sunday morning wake up bombs

"Card schools" a troglodyte life style

Mr Sulsky's smart gas mask cases

Social status of gas masks   "Molotov breadbaskets"

Bessy Bray's shop – surviving shelter life

Sunday 15th September Fine with showers. Alarm sounded at noon and again tonight. Walked past the airport to Cockernhoe this evening: the BBC evening news reported that 165 German planes were claimed shot down today "so far".

Monday 16th September Raining all day, attended evening class tonight. Felt unwell, two warnings sounded this afternoon and again tonight.

Tuesday 17th September Did not go to work but spent the morning in bed with a high temperature and sore throat. Two bombs fell at Markyate last night and the warning has already sounded tonight.

Wednesday 18th September Missed work again. An air raid warning tonight lasted for 2 and three quarter hours.

Thursday 19th September Returned to work this morning: a warning from 3-15 to 4-15 p.m. and an hour spent in the X Block trenches; dull skies and rain.

Friday 20th September Several bombs dropped in the town in the early hours and a plane blew up in mid air. One warning tonight – heard "Bulldog Drummond" on the radio.

Saturday 21st September Cycled through Kings Walden, Preston, Hitchin and Letchworth in warm, sunny weather this afternoon – there were several air raid warnings tonight.

Sunday 22nd September Raining all day, played Monopoly with Ivor and Clarice this afternoon – the game was interrupted by three warnings.

As September dragged on, the number of air raid alarms increased both night and day, the wailing sirens became the background of our daily life and people began to spend most nights in their Anderson shelters; this night was no exception, the rain had fallen steadily all day, the path to the shelter was muddy and until night fell our family huddled in the shelter, listening to the drone of the bombers for several hours until an intense, flickering light followed by a tremendous detonation rocked the town. The minutes following the explosion were filled with shouted enquiries from shelter to shelter: "are you alright?" "where did it land?" A huge parachute mine we later discovered had exploded in Park Street, narrowly missing Vauxhall's tank shop and destroying most of the buses which had escaped the bombing of the Corporation garage on the 30th August. The little houses in Park Street and Manor Road areas presented a sorry sight the following day, with their roofs stripped of tiles, doors and windows shattered and over a hundred people homeless.

Yet another explosion shook us later that night when another parachute mine exploded, but this one fortunately in mid-air where it did no damage.

Monday 23rd September Attended evening class tonight; I am more or less committed to an engineering apprenticeship but still retain a fondness for art and the hope that one day a career in commercial art or design might be possible; with this in mind, I climbed the stairs to the top floor of the Technical College which was occupied by Luton Art School and discussed the possibility of starting evening classes in the coming Spring with Mr Cyril Skinner, the School's Principal.

Weather, fine and sunny, Mr Morris was away from work – perhaps he too is feeling the strain.

Tuesday 24th September Found a lot of shrapnel at work today lying in the roadways, including several large jagged fragments: the recent rain has rusted the metal, making them easier to spot amidst the rubble. A new hobby has emerged amongst the office boys. Last year it was conkers and this year it's shrapnel; my collection is kept in a cotton flour bag held in the drawer of my office desk and contains several really evil specimens which I delight in showing to my friends and comparing with theirs. Went to evening class tonight; there were several air raid alarms and several bombs fell, including two on the airport.

Wednesday 25th September A fine day with cloudless sky. The bombs which fell last night were parachute mines, one badly damaged some cottages by the road to Wigmore Hall and the other failed to explode and hung by its parachute, snagged in the roof girders of a hangar at Percival Aircraft Ltd at the airport. All work at Vauxhall was suspended for two hours and I was instructed by Mr Morris to go home and advise my mother and all our neighbours on St Anne's estate to open their windows to minimise the danger of flying glass should the mine explode.

Whilst on my errand the sirens sounded the alert and the vapour trail of a high flying Nazi reconnaissance aircraft passed overhead: the photographs he took that morning were published after the war and clearly show the airport, the Vauxhall plant and the bomb craters. The mine was finally removed from its precarious position in the roof by a Group of Home Guard and Police volunteers and was de-fused by a naval mine expert, Lieutenant Armitage. Their bravery was later recognised by the award of two George Medals, and details of the operation were published in "Luton at War" some years later.

There were several warnings tonight and heavy bombs were dropped at Lilley.

Thursday 26th September Fine all day, filled sandbags tonight and put some on our shelter, several bombs fell nearby.

Friday 27th September Dad doped some sandbags with preservative and we filled some tonight – no bombs dropped. 133 German planes claimed today.

During the daylight hours the sky was filled with the incessant droning of the tiny yellow Miles Magisters, as trainee pilots practised takeoff and landings at the airport on the high ground to the East, but Luton's airfield was also briefly the home of a Fairey Battle bomber, a survivor of the single engined, under powered, under armed machines, squadrons of which were almost wiped out in the May retreat and which now appeared infrequently over Vauxhall. Our greatest frustration and

The Vauxhall Plant and Luton Airport seen from a Nazi reconnaissance plane on the morning of Wednesday 25th September. Home Guard and Police volunteers struggled to free a large parachute mine, dropped during the night and snagged in the roof girders of a Percival Aircraft Ltd hanger on the airport: the mine was eventually defused by a naval mine expert Lieut. Armitage; two George medals were awarded to those involved.

anger, however, was aroused by the Boulton Paul Defiant, a sad outmoded fighter plane equipped with a turret but no forward firing guns, which would take off into the evening sky just as the sirens were sounding and "Jerry" was overhead and return serenely some two hours later without, as far as we knew, firing a shot in anger.

Saturday 28th September Weather fine, did some homework this afternoon and later walked into town to buy paints and brushes at Cox's in Wellington Street. Two alarms tonight but no bombs fell.

Sunday 29th September Got up late this morning and walked to Wardown Museum with Clarice this afternoon. There were many air raid alarms tonight.

Monday 30th September Many air raid warnings throughout the day and night: attended evening class but arrived very late due to an alarm.

As Winter approached, the sweltering heat of Summer, the buckets of Horlicks and Roses lime juice became a distant memory. The weather was colder with long spells of rain and wind, and the long hours huddled in Vauxhall's concrete tunnels or our garden shelter were dreary, cold and miserable. Almost every night or part of the night during the next three months were spent in our Anderson shelter; only when enemy activity slacked off or when weather conditions made further attacks unlikely did we crawl into our beds in the hope of a few hours sleep before the morning trek down the hill to our work in the plant and brother Ivor to his school.

Tuesday 1st October Went to engineering drawing class tonight, spent the night in the air raid shelter.

Wednesday 2nd October Spent the night in the shelter.

Thursday, 3rd October Spent most of the day in the air raid shelter and did no work, stayed in the shelter all night.

Friday 4th October Walked into the town centre after work and collected a new suit from Burton's; the air raid sounded and I sought refuge with many others in a public shelter in Park Street. Tried on my new suit tonight and then followed the family to the shelter for yet another night cramped and cold. In 1940 the "teenager" had still to be invented; there were no teenage hair styles, music, clothing or pastimes, little leisure and no "leisure wear"; baseball caps, trainers, tracksuits and lycra pants were in the unimagined future and young people, childhood left behind them at fourteen, became replicas of their mothers and fathers, the girls in prim blouses and skirts and the boys in sober suits, collars and ties.

Saturday 5th October Shovelled more earth onto the shelter in the afternoon. Dad bought a chicken from a workmate, a rare treat for the family and a welcome addition to our meagre rations.

Sunday 6th October After a night of continuous alarms spent in the shelter, the "all clear" sounded in the early hours of the morning and, as it was raining and the cloud base was very low, we thought that another raid was unlikely and so retired to bed. Several hours later and half awake, I was aware of a startled shout from our neighbour, Jack Hardy, who was digging his garden and had seen a large twin engined aircraft low overhead with its engines idling and assumed it was "one of ours" preparing to land at the airport, when the concussion of its bombs roused us from our beds and a cloud of smoke and dust rose into the sky over Vauxhall.

Painted a picture of Kings Walden this afternoon and had roasted chicken for tea. Weather, rain and wind. Spent the night in the shelter.

Monday 7th October Ten bombs were dropped in yesterday's attack, three oil bombs and seven high explosives, but surprisingly little damage was done apart from one corner of Q Block and one which exploded at the rear of the works fire station, pitting the walls and shattering the canteen windows. Three of the H E bombs failed to explode and one of them, which rolled down the road between K Block and the canteen's bowling greens, caused great consternation to the commissionaire gate keeper. Those that did explode, however, provided valuable additions to my growing shrapnel collection. Evening class tonight.

Tuesday 8th October Pedalling past Q Block I found more shards of steel on the roadway and added them to my hoard; the cotton flour bag is now bulging with several pounds of once deadly fragments and is a great source of amusement to Arthur Fulcher, who regards my hobby as proof that I remain a silly schoolboy in spite of my Burton's suit. Attended evening class.

Wednesday 9th October After a night spent in the shelter, another warning early this morning made me late for work, which resulted in an ill tempered exchange with Mr Morris; the long hours of work, the endless hours in the shelters and the lack of sleep are sapping health and inducing in everyone the irritability that comes with exhaustion.

Thursday 10th October Some bombs were dropped near Kimpton tonight; I have just finished reading Harrison Ainsworth's "Dick Turpin's Ride to York". I am seeking to escape the present misery by immersing myself in Victorian romantic fiction in any spare moments.

Friday 11th October Mr Morris failed to turn up for work this morning, leaving the office in the charge of Bert Waller.

Saturday 12th October Cycling through Tea Green to Kings Walden this afternoon, I spotted a large patch of blackened grass and a small crater in a corner of Major Harrison's estate; after scrambling through a couple of hedges I found it to be the site of an oil bomb explosion, which yielded a large chunk of bomb casing (and my most impressive trophy to date), still reeking of its crude oil charge. Ivor's friend Roy Duncombe celebrated his birthday and visited us, travelling over from his grandmother's house at Dunstable.

Sunday 13th October Cycled through Hitchin, Letchworth and Baldock to Clothall to pick blackberries and then visited my old school friend Russell Rogers at his home in Norton village; the sirens sounded as we chatted and a high flying German plane passed overhead, trailing its vapour across the sky. Spent the night in the shelter.

Monday 14th October Weather, constant rain and low cloud; frequent air raid alarms throughout the morning and we spent hours in the X Block trenches. About noon a heavy explosion shook the ground, and word reached us a little later that a lone bomber had appeared from low cloud and dropped his bombs on some hat factories in Old Bedford Road; many women workers were killed. Attended evening class and spent the night as usual in the shelter.

Tuesday 15th October Mr Morris returned to work.

Wednesday 16th October Heard about a plan for staggered work hours; rain all day with a heavy downpour tonight. Spent the night in the shelter, very uncomfortable and wet.

Thursday 17th October Removed the mattress from the shelter and attempted to dry it out in front of the living room fire.

Friday 18th October Air raid alarm this afternoon – heard that "Robin Hood" starring Errol Flynn and Olivia de Havilland was coming to the Alma Cinema. Spent the night in the shelter and several bombs dropped "very near".

Saturday 19th October More bombs were dropped nearby.

Sunday 20th October Cycled though Lilley, Hexton and Pegsdon to Hitchin this morning; just past the Silver Lion pub where the Lilley Bottom road joins the Hitchin road, I noticed a large area of road surface whitened with chalk, and scrambling up the roadside bank I gazed into the most enormous crater I had ever seen. According to later estimates it was 54 feet across and 15 feet deep. In the afternoon I helped Dad construct some timber duck boards to keep our feet out of the puddles which had formed in the shelter as the recent rains seeped through the clay. Spent the night in the shelter and several more bombs fell.

Monday 21st October Several air raid alarms sounded during the day and the staff trudged along to the concrete lined tunnels on the waste ground to spend the next hour or two squatting on the slatted seats until the "all clear" sounded and we could resume our work once more. This almost daily routine created a new type of underground society, with familiar groups, or "card schools", gathering to play endless games of "solo" or "brag" and pass the long hours choking and coughing in the thick haze of tobacco smoke whilst the cards were dealt and played on a folding board resting on someone's knees: I resolved to embrace this new life style and on the way to evening class I purchased a pack of cards.

Half a year had passed since I had plodded up the slope from Kimpton Road's W Block gate, apprehensive, bewildered and unsure what the future held, to become a very junior member of the "Skipper's" crew and to learn something of life and Vauxhall Motors: so that I now recognised the route numbers scrawled on the yellow internal mail envelopes at a glance and could mount the departmental bike and deliver the mail to whichever area manager, engineer or foreman it was intended for without a second thought. Every block, workshop and office was now familiar territory for me and even blindfolded I could have guessed my location by smell alone: newly sawn oak where truck sides and tailgates were made, rubber and cellulose paint in K Block, cyanide in B Block, lard oil in P Block and, most familiar of all, our own records office where the heady fumes of methylated spirit from Mick Whiteley's "Ormig" copying machine was a constant presence.

Even vast sums of money were now entrusted to me when I was sent to the wages office cashier for cash when Mr Thursby or Mr Johnson was about to depart for Sheffield or Birmingham, and I would return with twenty or twenty five £1 notes (six months wages for me) carefully lodged in my jacket's inner pocket.

Tuesday 22nd October Dad and I put the wooden floor back into the shelter tonight – mist and rain all day. One of the lugs on my gas mask tin had come adrift, so I took it into work to have it spot welded into position. In the two years since the masks were issued their flimsy cardboard boxes had fallen apart, to be replaced by more robust containers of metal or leather; in the case of our family, cylindrical tin canisters with a screw-on lid and carried on a cord slung from the shoulder.

Thursday 24th October Today I received a small increase in wages as I had been six months employed by Vauxhall. Walked into town after work and had my hair cut by Charlie Inglis at his establishment in Park Street, then to Mr Sulsky's leather goods, camping and outdoor wear shop in Church Street to buy a leather strap for my gas mask tin. Mr Sulsky was a dapper gentleman of Russian or Polish Jewish origin who occupied one of a row of shops between Bill Johnson's café on the Park Square corner and the Wheatsheaf pub which faced the Masonic Hall.

Sulsky's could supply anything in leather – trouser belts, wallets, dog leads and collars, leather gaiters for farmers, elbow patches for teachers, and ladies' handbags: the disintegration of the government issue cardboard boxes provided Mr Sulsky with a business opportunity which he now grasped, offering a line of smart gasmask carriers made from khaki canvas with leather trim, shoulder straps and a press-studded flap for speedy access.

The universal civilian gas mask came in three distinct types and defined one's status in wartime society; firstly the children's "Mickey Mouse" mask in brightly coloured rubber and the much coveted civil defence pattern issued to ARP wardens, first aid workers and rescue squads and carried in a canvas haversack: this model, like the children's, was of moulded rubber with "bug eyed" individual eye pieces and an exhaust valve fitted over the nose. The rest of the population however, had a vastly inferior, cheaper "pig snout" model which, unlike the warden's mask, had a single window of flexible plastic which steamed up with condensed breath after three or four minutes, causing the wearer to blunder into other wearers and all objects, static or moving. For cheapness of manufacture the one way valve was dispensed with and exhaled breath merely blew out where rubber met cheek and chin with an embarrassing "raspberry" sound; as my friend Arthur Fulcher observed – when a group of people donned their masks at the same time, the resulting noise resembled "a farting contest in the backroom of a pub", a competitive sport which I was assured was still enjoyed in the wilder parts of Norfolk.

Friday 25th October Many incendiary bombs were dropped on the town tonight including a "Molotov breadbasket", a container timed to explode in mid air and scatter a hundred or more one kilogram fire bombs over a wide area; it was named after the Soviet Premier Molotov by the Finns when the Russian bombers used it with devastating effect on the mainly timber built Finnish towns during the Soviet/Finnish war nine months previously. Ours burst in the air with a brilliant chandelier effect, followed by the sound of scores of minor explosions and the glow of fires in the direction of Stopsley. Later that night we were aroused by the explosion of yet another breadbasket, and this time the fire glowed red as Lye's dye works near Wardown Park blazed into the night sky.

The flatulent model. The standard government issue "pig snout" civilian gas mask and its flimsy cardboard carrier, millions of which were distributed just before the outbreak of war and modified in June 1940 by the addition of a Contex filter secured to the snout with adhesive tape to frustrate Hilter's latest weapons of mass destruction. For cheapness, an exhaust valve was not included in the design and exhaled breath merely blew out where rubber met cheek and chin with an embarrassing "raspberry" sound, the cause of much ribald humour.

Saturday 26th October Worked until 11.30 a m and went with Clarice to see Errol Flynn and Olivia de Havilland in "Robin Hood" at the Alma Cinema this afternoon. We spent some hours in the shelter tonight and in the early hours of the morning, cold and sleepy, we retired indoors, where seated on kitchen chairs we huddled with elbows on knees over the last embers of our living room fire. Suddenly I was aware of a blow on my forehead and the smell of soot; now wide awake I realised that, overcome with fatigue, I had fallen into the fireplace but no harm done. I cycled to Kings Walden with Ivor the following afternoon with only a slight graze on my head to prove it was not just a bad dream.

Sunday 27th October Weather fine in the morning, cloudy in the afternoon. There were many alarms early in the night but it was quiet after midnight.

Monday 28th October The Italian army invaded Greece today. There was an air raid alarm this morning and several tonight – weather fine and cold.

Tuesday 29th October There was an air raid alarm at twenty to five and a few warnings early in the night; honed my card playing skills by playing with Ivor this evening.

Thursday 31st October Took my playing cards to work and spent most of the afternoon in the trenches putting my cards to good use – very heavy rain most of the day: did not go into our shelter tonight.

Friday 1st November More card playing; recovered my pack of cards which I had mislaid during yesterday's session. Mum bought me a new tie; several alarms tonight.

Soldiers and passing civilians watch a Bedford MW 15 cwt. truck put through its paces in Wardown Park's boating lake.

Saturday 2nd November Played whist tonight with Mum and Dad; we did not go out to the shelter – wind and heavy rain continues.

Called at Bessy Bray's shop on the corner of Devon Road and Rutland Crescent and bought a bar of chocolate: Bessy sold tobacco, sweets, grocery and household items: her shop was a neighbourhood general store and meeting place where news and gossip was exchanged and information gathered and passed on; where did last night's bombs fall, anyone killed, what damage was done and where can non-rationed food be procured? Bessy's brother, Eddie Jaques, an inspector in Vauxhall's gear shop, lived at Ampthill and kept livestock, so the occasional rabbit or hen would find its way to the shop to be eagerly snapped up by a grateful customer. Her customers often sought remedies for coughs and runny noses, afflictions which plagued almost everyone, and suggestions were offered on how to survive the cold in the Anderson shelters which ranged from knitted balaclava helmets and mittens to hotwater bottles and lighted candles placed under inverted clay plant pots; any idea to ease our present discomfort was eagerly taken up and tried out. A big factor in our plight was the condensation which formed on the cold steel roof and walls of the shelter and steadily dripped on the people beneath; to overcome this we took pieces of old towelling or any absorbent rags with us, wiping the steel at regular intervals and wringing out the water into a bucket.

So constant was the nightly drone of the bombers that people, unnerved by rare periods of silence, subconsciously braced themselves for unexpected horrors, whilst the distinctive irregular beat of their engines was recognised by every school age child and hailed by shouts of "that's a Jerry". Arthur Fulcher, whose old soldier's gallows humour had been honed to perfection on the Western Front, opined that the rhythm spelt out the threat "one for you y'bugger – one for you y'bugger", endlessly repeated, and was a fiendish but futile Nazi plot to destroy our morale: true or false, Arthur's wording fitted the engine's beat to perfection.

CHAPTER SEVEN

Smoke screen, bombs and exhaustion

November–December 1940

More bombs blast Luton Ear plugs issued
Chamberlain dies Middle aged and elderly suffer
Awful night of the Coventry raid
A proper smoke screen at last
Vauxhall's chirpy apprentices
Spotter alarms and surface shelters

Monday 4th November Several alarms during the day and hours spent in the trenches, weather dull and heavy rain all day.

Tuesday 5th November We went into the shelter tonight "but it was very wet", several bombs were dropped in the town, the flashes reminding me of happier peacetime Guy Fawkes nights; we later heard that the Dunstable Road and Beech Hill area had been hit with a big crater in the roadway, and a fire sprang up in Henry Brown's timber yard near the Odeon cinema.

Wednesday 6th November There were several alarms during the day, one at lunchtime which caused me to be late for work this afternoon; several long alarms tonight – very heavy rain all day.

Thursday 7th November Spent the night in the shelter, heard on the radio that Mr Chamberlain is seriously ill.

Saturday 9th November Many warnings this afternoon and tonight, collected a pair of rubber ear plugs from the St Anne's ARP post as it is believed that the latest poison gas devised by Hitler's scientists can attack through the ears, so as well as being rendered sightless by steamed up perspex we are now to be deaf also. It was announced on the radio that our former Prime Minister, Neville Chamberlain, had died – news that was received by most people with indifference rather than sadness.

Sunday 10th November Cycled through Kings Walden and Gosmore to Hitchin this morning, was caught in a heavy rainstorm and thoroughly soaked. Played whist tonight and there were several alarms. A great earthquake was reported in Rumania.

Monday 11th November Bought a poppy to remember the dead of the first Great War. Several alarms during the day, raining and windy, but we had a peaceful night.

Tuesday 12th November Had a row with "Norman" (Mr Morris), due no doubt to my misplacing one of the multitude of different forms in the complicated filing system which was my responsibility, but also a symptom of the weariness and tension affecting everyone.

Today was Dad's fifty-sixth birthday and Ivor and I bought him some of his favourite cigarettes, a brand called "Tennessee Whiffs" which were sold loose by Bavister's, a traditional tobacconists in Park Square and indulged in by him only on special occasions. If the present conditions were hard for us youngsters, how much more so were they for the ailing, the middle aged and elderly? Dad was working long hours of overtime in the evenings and weekends, often returning home to eat a hasty meal

Our Devon Road dugout. Searchlights at Offley and Butterfield Green sweep the sky with Jack Hardy's shed and the houses in Norfolk Road as a backdrop. Dad and I spent every spare moment heaving lumps of red clay and flint onto the shelter's roof, and a week later we constructed a blast wall of earth filled boxes and sandbags to shield the entrance. We and all our neighbours had taken Churchill's warning seriously and now seemed obsessed with a determination to burrow deeper into the earth like human moles.

and spend a sleepless night before facing another day at his toolmaker's bench.

Mother was three years younger than Dad and her health was already failing; terrified by the bombing and worried for her family and the future, she suffered from rheumatism and high blood pressure and would not live to see the war's end.

On clear nights when stiff limbs and the numbing dampness of the shelters drove us out to seek relief by walking about and stamping our feet, Dad, Ivor, Clarice and myself would gather with our neighbours Bill Creighton, Jack Hardy and Alf Hill to stand on the path to St Anne's factory gate to gaze at the twinkling shell bursts over London, the distant thunder and lightening flash of bombs, the pulsating red glow reflected from the clouds thirty miles away, and each one of us silently swore that one day the Nazis would be paid back a hundredfold in their own coin.

Thursday 14th November "There was a great air raid on Coventry tonight, many German aircraft passed over".

We took to our Anderson shelter in the early evening, huddled together and cold, with teeth chattering as the ceaseless drone of the bombers' engines continued for hours; the night was clear with a full moon, and the thick hoarfrost rimed the sandbags at the shelter's entrance as we peered out: a short pause in the droning and then the throb of the returning fleet kept us in the shelter until the "all clear" near daybreak, when we emerged bleary eyed and half frozen.

Friday 15th November Sunny with heavy frost and sun shining through the mist. "Many high explosive bombs were dropped nearby and in Luton tonight".

Saturday 16th November Lorry drivers delivering castings and components from the Midlands bring news of Coventry City cordoned off and dark stories of homeless thousands, soup kitchens and mass graves, arousing apprehension that Luton could be the Luftwaffe's next target.

In spite of all this horror, our thoughts were turning to the approaching Christmas season and prompted me to buy Christmas cards this afternoon. "One bomb was dropped in Luton tonight."

Sunday 17th November Cycled through Kings Walden, Hitchin and

Letchworth to visit my friend Jack Taylor. Passing down Crawley Green Road towards the Somerset Tavern, a neat gap was evident in the line of houses high on the embankment where the house and all its contents had been blasted down the slope and into the road during Friday night's attack. Took my dinner of sandwiches with me and went out with Jack, arriving back home at six o'clock. "It was a peaceful night".

Monday 18th November Mother raided her precious stock of dried fruit to bake Christmas cakes today. "We had a very quiet night".

Tuesday 19th November Weather dull and raining at times, several bombs fell nearby tonight. Bought some chestnuts for sister Clarice from one of my fellow office lads and she roasted them on the living room fire tonight between alarms.

Wednesday 20th November Many German aircraft passed over tonight and we did not get to bed until half past one.

Thursday 21st November Walked down Crawley Green Road after work and bought a copy of Picture Post, before spending some hours in the shelter.

Friday 22nd November More air raid warnings and we returned to the shelter tonight. Shortly after the devastating attack on Coventry and its industries, it apparently dawned on someone in authority that a large industrial town like Luton, an important centre of munitions production, was likely to suffer the same fate. It was therefore decided to resurrect the idea of a smoke screen to conceal the town and its factories but with a hopefully more effective scheme than the amateur "smoke bricks in the grate" fiasco which had failed so dismally in August.

A unit of the Army's Pioneer Corps known as a "Smoke Company"

Bomber's moon. Soldiers of the Pioneer Corps Smoke Company prepare Devon Road's oil fuelled smoke generators for action, some of the thousands of "smoke pots" which lined the streets of Luton, enveloping factories, streets and homes in dense stinking smoke. With the Vauxhall boundary just fifty yards behind the houses on the right, the St. Annes estate's smoke screen helped to conceal the plant on moonlit nights. Environmental pollution was of little concern to people in the desperate days of 1940, but none-the-less, the army's efforts were far more effective than Luton Council's fiasco of the 19th and 20th August when their tar and woodchip bricks burned in household grates produced nothing more than a smelly haze over the town.

suddenly appeared on our streets and installed twenty five thousand smoke generators placed in pairs about ten yards apart on the edge of the pavements; these novelty items of street furniture, which were soon dubbed "smoke pots", had a cylindrical tank surmounted by a chimney with a circular cap or baffle plate to hide the flames within from the bombers above and were fuelled by crude oil which produced huge volumes of stinking black smoke, contaminating houses, clothing and people with a greasy coating of filth.

The troops of the Smoke Company lived in a Nissan hutted encampment on open land between Crawley Green and Eaton Green Roads and it was here that their oil stores, trucks and equipment were kept. Soldiers were often seen in the daytime, with blackened faces, clad in leather jerkins and filthy denims, replenishing the oil tanks and cleaning soot from the chimneys; everyone felt sorry for them as it was surmised that when they joined the Army they never imagined a future patrolling the streets of Luton in a squad of chimney sweeps.

On clear, moonlit nights when the smoke pots were ordered into action, the soldiers drove through the streets, dropping off small detachments to light them, section by section and street by street, until a muffled roaring filled the night and houses, pubs, churches and factories were all engulfed. Sometimes accumulated soot would ignite or a fuel tank overheat and a rogue smoke pot would erupt with flames shooting skywards – usually as a bomber droned overhead, and shouted orders, curses and the clatter of ammunition boots were heard as soldiers rushed along Devon Road or Rutland Crescent to invert the baffle plate on the chimney top and snuff out the flame.

Saturday 23rd November Bought a flagon of sweet cider from the Hart Lane off licence and gave a book to young Marie Creighton. I made a label for my most prized piece of shrapnel, the large fragment of oil bomb found in Kings Walden Park, recording its date and location, and hung the ugly souvenir on my bedroom wall, much to mother's disgust.

"Had a very peaceful night".

Wednesday 27th November I walked into town after work, bought Royal Sovereign pencils and blotting paper and spent the evening practising old English gothic script. A small one kilowatt Belling electric fire was delivered today; this should prove a great comfort and a very welcome source of warmth when we emerge from the shelter, numb and half frozen.

Friday 29th November The weather clear and frosty, a bomb fell nearby tonight and we spent some time in the shelter. A large wart which had grown on a knuckle of my left hand came in contact with some solid object, partially unseating it and causing it to bleed profusely tonight.

The destruction of the August bombing had by now been largely repaired, with only the scars of chipped walls and shrapnel holes to remind us of the event, and the previous Spring intake of sixteen year old boys and my erstwhile office colleague and mentor Trevor Dean had long since settled into the life of engineering apprentices; on my daily errands around the plant, I often met two or three of them, usually on the hill between W Block and V Block when they were returning from the steel stores in X Block with a heavy load of steel bars tied to a low trolley, with roller bearings for wheels, and hanging on to a restraining rope like grim death to prevent it careering down the slope towards Kimpton Road. I would chat with them as they dragged their trolley through Q Block lorry park to the open doors of the Apprentice School workshops. They seemed to me to wear their baggy boiler suits with a certain cocky pride and swagger, with oily rags, tools and lumps of cotton waste stuffed into their pockets and exuding a cheery camaraderie to all and sundry; how I envied them and yearned for the day when I could join this brotherhood of the boilersuit and put behind me my years of servitude as an office boy and general dogsbody.

Saturday 30th November A sunny day with very heavy frost. Seasonable weather which reminded me that Christmas was fast approaching and caused me to buy more Christmas cards. "We had a very peaceful night".

Sunday 1st December Fine weather and frost persists; cycled to Letchworth and walked down to Nortonbury Mill and the River Ivel with my friends Jack Taylor and Russell Rogers – arrived home at five thirty. "There was only one short warning tonight".

Monday 2nd December There was another short warning tonight and Mrs Creighton came over for a comforting chat with mother; Bessie, a frail woman in poor health, is feeling the strain of the bombing and the nights in the shelter more than most.

Tuesday 3rd December There were two alarms during the day and a high flying German reconnaissance plane was seen: another warning tonight and several bombs were dropped near Toddington which shook the house.

Wednesday 4th December There was a long "alert" which kept us in the shelter for most of the night as many bombers droned overhead, doubtless on their way to attack a city in the Midlands. My attendance at evening classes had ceased since the last week of October due to exhaustion and the constant interruption of the sirens; concentration and homework I found impossible in these conditions, and studying for the future seemed pointless when it was uncertain whether we had a future at all.

After almost four months of incessant air raid alarms, the Government realised that the hundreds of hours spent idling in the trenches and the consequent loss of munitions to the war effort was too great to sustain, indeed, Vauxhall's workforce of thousands often spent entire days or nights reading, smoking or playing cards, with the assembly lines stopped, the machine shops and offices deserted. To remedy this it was decided to introduce a "spotter" system, with a lookout tower of scaffolding erected on St. Anne's Hill near the plant boundary fence with the town cemetery, with a mast and a red and white signal drum rising from its platform. The tower was manned night and day and, from their elevated vantage point, the spotters had a clear view over the entire plant and all the horizon from the airport in the East to Stockwood Park in the West: in addition to their binoculars they had a direct telephone link with the Royal Observer Corps and, when they judged the enemy were heading our way and an attack was imminent, the "take cover" signal was given, a series of shrill "pips" on the works' Tannoy sound system, causing everyone to cease work and bolt for cover.

For many workers the existing shelters were too distant for a warning of one or two minutes, so surface shelters were built alongside and sometimes inside offices and workshops; these were windowless brick boxes with a concrete roof, far too flimsy to survive even a near miss, but proof we were assured against splinters and blast, though few took the assurances seriously and thankfully they were never put to the test.

They offered little more comfort than our familiar underground trenches, with the same buttock-numbing hard seats and dim electric lighting, but thankfully the air was warmer and they lacked that bone-chilling dampness, offering a slightly more congenial environment for the "card schools" that flourished everywhere.

CHAPTER EIGHT

Our meagre Christmas

December 1940

Christmas preparations   A drastic cure for a sore knuckle
Steel sheet replaces window glass
My fifteenth birthday   Mr Johnson's chicken
Mr Williams – canteen manager
The notorious Vauxhall rissole
Christmas eve – M. D. Bartlett's Tannoy message
One day of peace and goodwill and back to work
Great London fire raid   New Year's Eve reverie

Friday 6th December Had lunch in the canteen and bought a desk blotter; these were neatly boxed, surplus, peacetime sales promotion gifts in ivory coloured bakelite with a blue and silver enamelled Vauxhall badge; a handsome object but fairly useless gift, now on sale at our canteen shop and being snapped up by eager buyers with Christmas in mind. One alarm during the day and another tonight.

Saturday 7th December Weather sunny and very cold; walked into town this afternoon and bought a colour box of oil paints complete with turps, palette and brushes at William Harold Cox's photographic studio and art materials shop in Wellington Street. No alarms tonight.

Sunday 8th December Sunny and very cold; went for a long cycle ride through Letchworth, Weston and Cottered, arriving home at five o'clock. There were several alarms tonight, and between alerts we gathered at our usual spot by St Anne's gate to gaze at "great activity over London".

Monday 9th December No warnings tonight; Ivor and I made paper chains of coloured gummed paper strips as we did at school; we intend to keep Christmas in the traditional way as far as possible and in spite of the bombs.

Tuesday 10th December I tried to obtain one of the fancy desk

By December 1940, just 22 weeks after design work began, prototypes were produced, and, as seen here, were undergoing tests in the mud of the Luton Hoo testing grounds with a dummy turret fitted.

blotters for Clarice from the canteen shop at lunchtime but found to my disgust they were sold out. The large wart on my left hand was almost knocked off tonight, bleeding freely and secured now by only its roots.

Wednesday 11th December With Mr Morris's permission I visited the Works surgery to seek treatment for my hand and its pendant wart. The nursing sister in charge is a formidable lady sporting a silver buckled belt, a starched collar and a brisk, efficient manner; she sat me on a bed, proclaimed that in her view most men were wimps, ordered me to look away, and, with a deft snip of her surgical scissors, severed

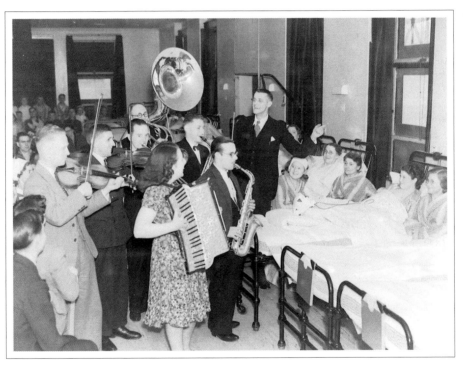

Saturday 14th December 1940. Musicians of Vauxhall's orchestra, led by their musical director, Fred Green, entertain patients and staff at the Luton and Dunstable Hospital with a concert of Christmas Carols. This was also the occasion for the presentation of a piano donated by Vauxhall in response to a Luton News appeal.

my wart. She painted the wound with a bright orange antiseptic and bound it with so many layers of bandage that my left hand resembled a white boxing glove. Back at the office I was received with murmurs of sympathy by the secretaries and typists, but Arthur Fulcher regarded me with an old soldier's knowing grin; his survival skills had been learned in the trenches and he recognised a malingerer when he saw one. At lunchtime the sirens sounded and my diary notes: "A terrific amount of German aircraft passed over tonight". Weather sunny, heavy frost tonight.

Thursday 12th December I visited the surgery to have my hand inspected and re-dressed this morning and confirmed Arthur's suspicions when I returned to work, my sore knuckle covered by only a light bandage and small sticky plaster. I wrote a letter and sent Christmas greetings to my old headmaster, Mr Haysman, tonight. Heavy frost and frequent warnings all night, which kept us shivering in the shelter.

Sunday 15th December I cycled to the villages of Clothall and Weston and cut some holly for Christmas, stuffed it into my saddlebag and cycled home in time for tea at half past five. Wrote a letter to my old form teacher, Bernard Youngman, tonight – there were several air raid alarms.

Thursday 19th December As a safety measure, it has been decided to remove all Vauxhall's window glass which has survived the bombing and replace it with panes of sheet steel, resulting in dozens of teams in safety gloves and goggles, laboriously chiselling out hardened putty and littering floors with broken glass.

Friday 20th December Received a Christmas card from my old friend Russell Rogers this morning; whilst busy at my desk filing the endless

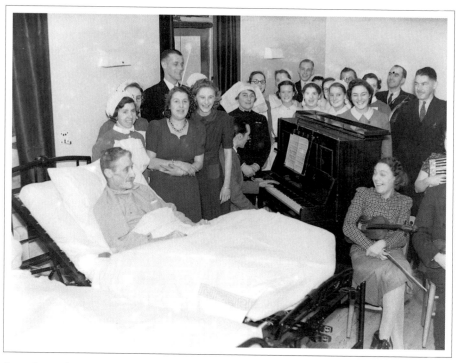

Saturday 14th December 1940 and Vauxhall musicians try out the newly donated piano as patients and nursing staff at the Luton and Dunstable Hospital gather round. The dark suited man far right is Ken Smith, General Secretary of VM Recreation Club, later to be commissioned Major Smith officer commanding Vauxhall's J Company Home Guard.

orders and planning sheets, I became aware of Mr Morris quietly moving among the typists and other staff and the chink of coins as he took a collection to be shared amongst the office boys. There were several warnings tonight and the weather was bitterly cold, but in spite of the cards, the holly, the paperchains and the valiant efforts of friends and family, it was almost impossible to re-create the Christmas magic of previous years.

Saturday 21st December Walked into town this afternoon and bought myself a gabardine raincoat at Burton's and searched the bookshops in vain for a copy of Dickens' "Christmas Books" in the fond hope that it would remind me of Mr Poppy and his readings of "A Christmas Carol" and conjure the lost spirit of the season of goodwill; a hard task, when the air raid sirens wailed again and repeated the warnings through the night hours.

Sunday 22nd December Cycled to Nortonbury and Baldock in the dull, bitterly cold weather this morning and made a drawing of Old Warden tonight: we had a peaceful night.

Monday 23rd December My fifteenth birthday and the weather remains bitterly cold; Mr Morris instructed me to go to the canteen and pick up a chicken for our manager, Mr Johnson; I was to introduce myself to Mr Williams, the canteen manager, explain my errand and return to X Block with the Christmas bird without delay. Eagerly anticipating my share of Friday's collection, I cycled down the hill and parked my bike near the canteen's back entrance and next to the large bins which held kitchen waste destined for pig swill. Passing through the loading dock where supplies were delivered, I had my first sight of catering on an industrial scale; huge steam-heated cauldrons set in the tiled floor and vast stainless steel ovens exuded a fug of warm humidity and a rather unappetising smell of cooking. This reminded me that I was in the birthplace of the notorious "Vauxhall rissole", a strange square cake which appeared to consist of minced bacon rinds, onion, bread, potatoes and seasoning, whose chief merit was that it was cheap and filling and, when served with peas, mash or chips and awash in glutinous brown gravy, was just about edible; rumour had it that the jealously guarded recipe was covered by the Official Secrets Act and

right In spite of the sirens and bombs there were Christmas Pantomimes at the Grand Theatre and the Alma, with Charlie Chaplin's "The Great Dictator" coming soon to the Palace Cinema in Mill Street to mock Hitler and raise our spirits.

TO-DAY *and* ALL NEXT WEEK

PERFORMANCES THREE TIMES DAILY

2.30–5.30–7.45

Grand Annual Christmas Pantomime

Little Red Riding Hood

With Strong Cast Of Pantomime Favourites

—USUAL PRICES—

Reserved 1/3 to 3/-

Unreserved 6d. to 2/6

Children Bring Your Parents
Parents Bring Your Children

To A Real Family Christmas Pantomime

The ALMA ABC THEATRE LUTON·PHONE 1901

TWICE DAILY
2.0 (Doors Open 1.30)
6.30 (Doors Open 6.0)

BOOK NOW! BOOK NOW! BOOK NOW!

For The Finest Pantomime Ever Seen In Luton!

MOTHER GOOSE

ARTHUR LOWRIE AS "MOTHER GOOSE." OLGA MAY AS "COLIN." GEORGE BARTON AS "JACK." Irene Ashton as "Jill." Connie Thorne as Fairy Queen." Sam Gosling as "The Golden Goose." Hal Collins as "The Mayor." Specialities by SAM LINFIELD & CO.; The Imperial Ballet; The Warren Dene Girls—"Sunshine" Babies; Stupendous Transformation Scene—"Fairy Fountains"

MAKE UP YOUR PARTIES AND BOOK NOW!

Prices:- 1/6 2/- 2/6 3/- 4/-

SPECIAL MATINEE PRICES FOR CHILDREN

PALACE, LUTON (G.B.)

TO-DAY.— Continuous from 2.0 — 9.45

WILLIAM HOLDEN, MARTHA SCOTT in

OUR TOWN (A)

Also LEE TRACY in MILLIONAIRES IN PRISON (A)

NEXT WEEK

THE CRAZY GANG in GASBAGS

Soon:- CHARLES CHAPLIN — THE GREAT DICTATOR

A.R.P. Don't come on Saturday if you can come before

At Watford on Christmas morning.

WATFORD 2
Lewis (H) 2 (1 penalty)
LUTON 2
Lutterloch, Gager

LUTON—Coen; Gager, Dunsmore, Campbell, Hunt, J Forsyth; J Dowers, Laing, Duggan, Lutterloch, Perrins.

WATFORD — McHugh; Harris, Lewis (J), P Giddins, Woodward, R King, Jones, Barnett, Lewis (H), R Williams, Brown.

Referee—K D Eames, Watford.

The Town players complained bitterly of the referee's handling of the game, especially in the second half, but generally the football was good, the Town forwards in the second period especially playing cleverly though missing chances.

Luton had the better of the exchanges in the early stages, and McHugh made several good saves. However, a goal came after a clever movement, in which Lutterloch, Perrins, Laing and Dowers had a part, and LUTTERLOCH scored with a strong shot which glanced off Lewis (J), though it would have registered had it not touched the player. Coen had to make several saves, but loose play in the Town defence enabled Brown and LEWIS (H) to get through, and the latter scored with a grand shot as he fell. Shortly afterwards Watford were awarded a penalty when Hunt robbed Lewis (H) near goal, but Jones's spot kick went wide. Half-time:

WATFORD 1
LUTON 1

Luton had much the better of play in the second half, and McHugh made grand saves. Eventually a corner kick was cleared but GAGER, who had come forward, met the ball and drove in a surprise shot which McHugh could not reach in time, and Luton were ahead. Watford were kept busy for some time, and then in a breakaway Hunt received a centre on his chest, but the referee adjudged that he had handled and gave a penalty kick, from which LEWIS (H) equalised. Lutterloch missed an open goal in the closing stages, during which Watford were awarded many free kicks despite protests by the Town defenders.

At Luton on Christmas Day afternoon.

LUTON TOWN 4
Duggan (2), Dunsmore (penalty), Laing
WATFORD 1
Lewis (H)

Luton team as above, save Armes for Dowers and Smith (J R) for Perrins.

WATFORD — McHugh; Harris, Lewis (D), Lowe, Giddins, King, Jones, Barnett, Lewis (H), Williams, Brown.

Referee—W E Wood, Bedford.

As keenly fought as any game we have seen this season was the return game at Luton in the afternoon, and the Town were good value for success. The margin about represented the balance of play, though it may have exaggerated slightly the respective merits of the teams, for Watford's attack gave a lot of trouble, mainly due to the inspiration of Tommy Barnett. Watford's thrusts came chiefly through their wingers, and once more I thought that Gager and Dunsmore confidently and skilfully though [illegible] played gave the opposing wingers too much rope.

Town middle line also played very well indeed, Forsyth especially, and the attack worked smoothly, though still disposed to hang on to the ball much too long when they might have shot with success. Smith, the Millwall winger, and Armes, the Middlesbrough winger, gave some colour to the attack, and the rest of the line gave them plenty of work. Duggan was always the most dangerous man in front of goal.

Watford had something for which to thank McHugh, who made [illegible] all the time. Barnett [illegible] superior as an artist [illegible] rarely failed to make [illegible] the ball, and Jones started [illegible] fell away later. Williams [illegible] "Skiller" Williams, the old [illegible] goalkeeper, is a very young player.

TOWN PRESSURE

From the kick-off W[illegible] away, and Brown swung [illegible] across for Jones to [illegible] Smith led the reply, and [illegible] saved twice as the Town tried to rush the ball [illegible]. Armes soon found favour [illegible] crowd, and finished a [illegible] sending a foot wide. [illegible] were forced by the [illegible] Harris saved under the [illegible] McHugh had been beaten [illegible] from Forsyth. Duggan [illegible] clean through, but shot [illegible] the goalkeeper, and Wat[illegible] away, Hunt saving a [illegible] by quick tackling of Wil[illegible] in. Smith hesitated [illegible] might have shot with [illegible] a moment later a fine shot [illegible] same player was very [illegible] forced a corner and McH[illegible] brilliantly a header from [illegible] when Smith sent the ball [illegible] [illegible]

DUGGAN'S GOAL

[illegible]

THREE UP

[illegible]

Millwall Take Chances

VISITING LUTON TOWN on Saturday, MILLWALL ATHLETIC won by a margin of two goals. In some respects it was a lucky victory, for the visitors were defending for the greater part of the game, the Town backs frequently spending several minutes in the vicinity of the circle. However, the Millwall defence was strong and the forwards able to take openings quickly [illegible]

[illegible]

* * *

THE TOWN [illegible]

many of the canteen's customers claimed it to be England's secret weapon; what was beyond doubt, however, was that it produced awesome flatulence in its victims and great discomfort for their workmates.

A white overalled cook directed me to Mr Williams' office, a small glass panelled structure situated at the far end of the kitchen, where I announced the reason for my intrusion and was received with a grunt. Mr Williams, who dressed formally in a stiff collar, black jacket and striped trousers as any restaurant manager would, was a gentleman of immense proportions; his bulk filled the swivel chair behind his desk, where he reclined with laboured breathing like a stranded whale. Close by his left hand stood a large safe with its door ajar to reveal glimpses of Christmas fare within; poultry, wine and spirits and it was to the left that Mr Williams slowly swivelled and withdrew a plucked and drawn chicken encased in a paper bag.

Pedalling back to the Planning department with the chicken in the carrier basket, I recalled with sadness the turkey our family had feasted on last Christmas and the utter impossibility of obtaining even an old "boiling fowl" this year; my thoughts also turned to Mr Johnson and the daunting task he faced every day to plan the means to produce the tanks and the trucks so desperately needed by our soldiers, and so it was with scarcely a pang of envy that I handed over the chicken, with the heartfelt hope that he would enjoy every morsel and a restful and peaceful Christmas day.

In the evening I found a birthday card awaiting me from my old schoolmate Rusty Rogers and the family celebrated my birthday with a tin of Russian lobster, a favourite delicacy of mine which mother produced from her tiny stock of prewar "special" items, and a flagon of sweet cider from the Hart Lane off licence.

After the tea things were cleared away, we decorated the living room with paper chains and streamers, but it seemed the Luftwaffe would give us no respite for Christmas, as several times during the night and

A "Seasonal" Christmas Eve Pictorial front page, and two children emerge from their Anderson shelter to scan the sky for Santa and his sleigh, but more likely for Nazi bombers.

the early morning hours of Christmas Eve the siren's familiar howl
blared out over Luton.

Tuesday 24th December The atmosphere in the office was strangely
relaxed and jovial, with everyone, including Mr Morris, seeming to
conspire to create a festive spirit; the typewriters' clatter seemed less
busy than normal and Arthur Fulcher's cheerful, lengthy conversations
with the draughtsmen, as he issued drawings, did not attract the usual
disapproval from our boss. About mid-morning Mr Morris came round
with a tray containing the office boys' "Christmas boxes" – little buff
envelopes containing each boy's share of Friday's collection; I was
delighted to find that mine was fourteen shillings and sixpence – a
whole week's wages.

Arthur shared my pleasure when I told him of my good fortune and
fell into reminiscent mood, recalling with obvious joy Christmas times
of his own youth: the sumptuous festivities and the hordes of guests at
the great country houses, shoots over the estate's vast acres, the feasting,
drinking and room to room wanderings of his lordship's lecherous
guests; all of which was made possible by the efforts of an overworked
army of servants. Butler, housekeeper, head gamekeeper and head cook
managed however by underhand pilfering – or avoidance of waste, as
they cared to see it – to provide the servants with a choice of the finest
vintages and a Christmas dinner in no way inferior to his lordship's.

Work tapered off during the afternoon and about three o'clock the
Tannoy loudspeakers crackled into life as our Managing Director,
Charles Bartlett, thanked us for our efforts, sympathised with us for the
difficulties we had encountered in the past months and wished us all a
happy Christmas; shortly after the broadcast Mr Johnson emerged from
his office and toured the department to wish all his engineers, managers
and Mr Morris a happy Christmas; a bottle or two of sherry was
produced and discreetly passed around, and at half past five I climbed
the concrete steps at the rear of X Block to grope my way in the

darkness along the spoil heap path to St Anne's gate and our home in Devon Road.

Although tomorrow was to be our only holiday, I was determined to enjoy it to the full, starting tonight, and after tea we stoked up the fire, stuck holly behind the pictures, arranged Christmas cards on sideboard and mantelpiece, regaled ourselves with nuts, cake and wine and listened to a special Christmas "Kentucky Minstrels" show on our radio, meanwhile keeping our ears cocked for the sirens, but thankfully the evening and night passed without warnings.

Wednesday 25th December Christmas day was dull and cold with a thick mist hanging over St Anne's estate and Vauxhall: in the morning I tried, without success, a still life study of a lustre goblet with my newly acquired oil paints; we had a leg of lamb for dinner, followed by cider and port, and in the afternoon I walked into town attired in my new suit to see "The Sea Hawks" at the Savoy cinema. The day and evening passed peacefully with no sirens to disturb us.

Thursday 26th December Boxing Day and we returned to work with the atmosphere in the office subdued and quiet, as people struggled to put the unaccustomed luxury of a whole day of rest, ample food and undisturbed sleep behind them and resign themselves to the resumption of the now familiar routine of work and the dash to the trenches.

Aunt Ethel Hill, her son, cousin Clifford and his wife visited us today from their temporary home in Berkhamsted.

Saturday 28th December I cycled to Letchworth in the afternoon and finally managed to find and buy a copy of Dickens' "Christmas Books" at W H Smith's; no warnings tonight.

Sunday 29th December Cycled through Hitchin and Letchworth to Nortonbury Mill and then up the Great North Road towards Radwell, arriving home at half past five.

The sirens sounded this evening; we went to our shelter but, hearing no drone of bombers overhead, we emerged to join our neighbours standing mute in the path to St Anne's gate and gazing awestruck at the shell bursts and the terrible red sky which flickered and pulsated as London's old City centre burned around St Paul's; a sky of a more lurid colour than even those of September when the Docks and oil refineries burned. This great fire raid brought the realisation that fire could be a greater threat to lives and property than high explosive and brought about the formation of a fire guard and the creation of another wartime institution – that of "fire watching" – when by law every able-bodied

Unlike the standard steel helmet worn by the armed forces and Civil Defence, many thousands of this high domed helmet for Fire watchers were produced by Vauxhall's Press Shop, and here modelled by Colin Cook at his "Museum in the Garden". Colin is equipped with a primitive hand-operated stirrup pump and a long-handled scoop for dousing blazing magnesium incendiary bombs with sand or slag.

adult in Luton – unless exempt by other service – was compelled to register and be available to tackle the incendiary bombs. The aim was to ensure that no building was unattended by day or night; in practice it meant taking flask and sandwiches and spending a restless night on a hard bunk in a warehouse, office or church and, on reaching my

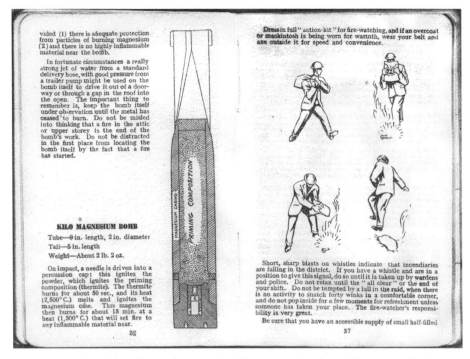

From a Fire Guards handbook, the one Kilo Magnesium bomb, and how to tackle it.

sixteenth birthday, I spent many such nights on watch in our X Block office and later in the Apprentice School classrooms. Our press shop also produced a special quaintly styled fire watcher's steel helmet which was issued to every Vauxhall employee and distributed in thousands across the country.

Tuesday 31st December **New Year's Eve** and by now Vauxhall had regained its usual pace, with engineers, draughtsmen and clerical staff, heads down, working hard, with convoys of finished trucks leaving the plant daily for army transport depots.

At this turn of the year my thoughts ranged back over the preceding months and the drastic changes in my life; from idle, carefree schoolboy to a tired war worker, an insignificant cog in a mighty war machine.

The naivety and optimism of my first weeks at Vauxhall in hindsight seemed incredible and those Spring days unbelievably distant. Sadly remembered also were our Vauxhall workmates and all the other good people of Luton laid to rest in their freshly dug graves in Luton's cemetery and churchyards, never to see this New Year.

Through all the Summer, Autumn and Winter months a remarkable transformation had taken place amongst the population of Luton, as the Civil Defence organisation was improved and extended and as the people became hardened to the grim realities of a way of life which was so drastically changed from that of twelve months before.

Thousands had enrolled in the A.R.P. as wardens, drivers, telephone operators or members of the heavy rescue squads: the Auxiliary Fire Service (AFS) augmented the Regular Fire Service and Vauxhall's Home Guard Company, now numbering several hundreds, was losing its amateur appearance, the denim overalls, armbands and workboots of the previous summer discarded in favour of khaki battle dress and army boots: its improvised weapons of the early days steadily replaced by World War One American P17 rifles and ammunition, arriving from U.S. arsenals along with ex Royal Flying Corps machine guns of the same vintage. Steel helmets and battle dress of varying colours became the most common attire, with many people wearing them to work, particularly if they had to report for duty that night. Ahead of us lay the unknown months of vile Winter weather, more bombings and nights of gasping in the filthy smoke; weeks of sickness when our poor diet and miserable life in the cold, damp shelters finally caught up with us; but on New Year's Eve we scoffed the last crumbs of the Christmas cake, drank the last drops of wine and retired to bed to enjoy a night of undisturbed sleep and awoke to a freezing and sunlit first day of January 1941.

CHAPTER NINE

New year — new hope

January–December 1941

Grim times – we still stand alone

Sickness strikes – Scarlet Fever and Flu

My skin turns yellow   The much envied barley sugar kid

Spring brings stirrings of hope

Joy! Two Nazi raiders down   The Deputy Fuehrer arrives

Russia attacked – our new ally   "Tanks for Russia" week

U.S. attacked – the Yanks are in

Yet another wartime Christmas   Feeding the pigs

Hitler is doomed

The feelings of optimism and hope that come with every New Year soon evaporated in the early months of 1941, which was, without a doubt, the most wretched of the War. The weather was foul, and the news from abroad was of seemingly endless disaster, whilst the ruins of the City of London, Coventry, and a score of our major cities, still smouldered; sporadic air raids continued, the shrill blasts of the "spotters" warnings on the works' Tannoy sending us scuttling to the trenches, whilst night after night the soldiers clattered down the streets and our smoke screen spluttered into action, blackening the snow on the pavements and smothering the town in oily filth, but worst of all, after almost twelve months, we still faced the Nazis alone.

Thursday 6th February A mood that was dogged, grim and miserable gripped one and all, and today, a day of heavy snow, sickness struck our family when Dad took to his bed with Flu and sister Clarice was taken to the Spittlesea Isolation Hospital suffering from Scarlet Fever.

Friday 14th February A parachute mine dropped in the night, missed Vauxhall and exploded harmlessly near the railway tracks to provide me with more shrapnel for my collection.

Wednesday 19th February The following Wednesday, after several days of feeling unwell, I collapsed unconscious at work to be taken home by the works' ambulance. Four days later, still feeling unsteady but preparing to return to work, I was horrified to see, reflected in the mirror, a face that was a strange shade of yellow, and, as brother Ivor cruelly observed, the whites of my eyes were the colour of "rotten eggs".

Monday 24th February The doctor was sent for and I was informed that I was suffering from Jaundice – the good news was that part of the cure was barley sugar, which mother obtained on prescription from Boots, and which made me the object of envy to everyone whose meagre sweet ration was long gone.

Tuesday 25th February "Heard this morning that mother's brother, Uncle Harry, has died".

As Spring advanced and the weather improved, the faintest stirring of hope was kindled: as month followed month and season followed season with no sight of the Nazi invasion fleet, the threat receded and a faint optimism spread; the whole of Europe from Arctic Norway to Greece was now conquered by the enemy, and even the wildest optimist could not imagine how victory could be won – but we had survived, Churchill and the Nation remained defiant, and it was almost a year since the remnants of our battered army had escaped from France.

Plant Manager, Reg. Pearson, guides Mr Churchill through a component machining area.
This photograph gives a good impression of the claustrophobic daytime working
conditions in the totally blacked-out workshops with all the lighting switched on.

16th March My health slowly returned and on Sunday in warm
  sunshine I cycled to Ivinghoe Beacon with Ivor and the following day
  returned to work after a break of four weeks. Nightly air raid alarms
  and smoke screens continued to harry us throughout March and April,
  and just before Easter our spirits received a great boost, when, as my
  diary noted:

Wednesday 9th April "Heard that a German bomber was shot down
  at Breachwood Green last night". And on the following day

Thursday 10th April "Another German plane was shot down at
  Breachwood Green last night".

Sunday 13th April Ivor and I cycled to the crash site at Bendish to rummage about in the charred wreckage for souvenir brass cartridge cases which had exploded in the heat, and then onto the grave of the second bomber which had hit the ground near Stagenhoe Park. We were further cheered to learn that one of the first bomber's crew, who had bailed out, was caught by a young seventeen year old Vauxhall apprentice and Home Guard, David Stedman, who lived at Ley Green Post Office.

Saturday 3rd May "Heard the Prime Minister speak tonight".

Thursday 8th May "Learned that 23 German planes were shot down last night".

Managing Director, Charles Bartlett, Winston Churchill and assorted officers admire a truck at the end of K Block assembly line.

Sunday 11th May "There was a terrible raid on London last night".

Monday 12th May "Herr Hess did a bunk today".
This was incorrect: Tuesday's newspapers revealed that Rudolf Hess landed near Glasgow in his Messerschmitt 110 on Saturday night, whilst London suffered the terrible raid which damaged Westminster Abbey, the Houses of Parliament and the British Museum; there was widespread speculation that he hoped to make contact with leading members of the establishment who were thought to favour a negotiated peace deal with Hitler.

Friday 16th May "Saw the King when he visited Vauxhall this afternoon". He was shown the first tanks to be built, and, accompanied

With an expression of grim satisfaction, Mr Churchill looks on as workers build a tank named after himself on Luton's Y Block assembly line.

by Charles Bartlett and Reg Pearson, toured the Y Block assembly line and later inspected tanks on the Luton Hoo test ground.

Tuesday 20th May Dad went to London's Moorfields Hospital to obtain a new glass eye.

Saturday 24th May Heard the awful news that the Hood has been sunk. Mum is not well tonight. "Her nose bled for a long time – got alarmed".

Mr Churchill, accompanied by Charles Bartlett and "top brass", inspects a Churchill tank in the Luton Hoo testing grounds; this early model was armed with the almost useless two pounder (pea shooter) gun, soon to be superseded by the six pounder, a superior weapon but still no match for the German panzers.

Sunday 25th May Saw a fire bomb demonstration at Vauxhall.

Tuesday 27th May Heard of the sinking of the Bismark.

Wednesday 28th May "Several big bombs fell nearby early this morning". The new QL 4 x 4 trucks are now rolling off the K Block assembly line in large numbers; many of them are QLBs – Bofors gun tractor units designed to haul the 40mm Bofors gun, accommodate the gun crew and all their equipment and ammunition; whilst their four wheel drive, high ground clearance and powerful winches ensure they

The date is 16th May 1941, barely eleven months since Vauxhall was asked to design and build the A22 heavy tank, and King George VI, accompanied by Charles Bartlett and Reg. Pearson, inspects the first Churchill tanks to come off the Luton assembly line.

can extricate themselves from deep mud or sand dunes. Hundreds of them are parked nose to tail alongside the test track in front of X Block and, as I pedal past them on my works' bike, I often try to imagine them in action.

Monday 2nd June – Whit Monday "Saw Arthur Askey in "The Ghost Train" at the Palace cinema this afternoon. Listened to the radio news bulletin tonight, we have quit Crete, things look very serious".

King George VI, accompanied by a senior tank Corps officer, Vauxhall's M.D. Charles Bartlett and company executives, inspects Churchill tanks in the Luton Hoo testing grounds in May 1941. The man in the white coat in the foreground is believed to be Experimental engineer H. A. (Bertie) Dean.

The Duke of Kent was also amongst the VIPs to visit the Luton Plant's Y Block to inspect the first Churchill tanks off the assembly line; seen here in RAF uniform, he was killed on active service just over a year later when his plane crashed off Scotland.

Sunday 22nd June On a brilliant hot and sunny day we heard that Hitler's massed divisions had surged into Russia on a huge front and it became clear why we had suffered no air raids for almost a month, and possibly explained Deputy Fuehrer Hess's trip to Glasgow. The feeling of relief was palpable; we no longer faced Hitler alone; only the USSR in the whole of Europe had the military might and industrial muscle to challenge the Nazis; almost overnight they became our heroes. The hostility of eighteen months before when they had attacked Finland was forgotten, and on the Sunday evening we gathered round our radios to hear Mr Churchill extend the hand of friendship and pledge our support.

Two soldiers of the Royal Tank Corps intently watch a Churchill MK IV tank undergoing tests in the water tank. The locomotive in the background is Vauxhall's very own shunting engine which ran on the rail siding in front of the swarf house.

Sunday 13th July A radio news bulletin told us of a Pact with the Soviet Union, a promise of mutual aid and a pledge that neither would sign a separate peace with Germany.

Sunday 24th August We listened to Churchill's speech.

Monday 25th August Britain and Russia invaded Iran to open and secure a Southern supply route.

Wednesday 27th August Today all Vauxhall employees were issued with a steel helmet; one of the quaintly-styled, high-domed models intended for fire watchers, and produced in their thousands in our Press shop; mine hung on a peg in the office along with my gas mask, ready for the dash to the trenches when the spotters' warning pips sounded.

Monday 8th September "Berlin was heavily bombed last night". When my errands took me through the Die Shop, I was intrigued to see from time to time a Churchill's rusty hull or turret hauled in from the Shoeburyness ranges where it was tested against various anti-tank weapons – both British and German. The army had recorded in white paint the calibre of every missile at its point of impact – the metal gouged and torn, with the smaller solid shot in many cases still embedded in the armour, but where the steel was blasted clean through, the hole was marked "88", indicating a shell from the fearsome German 88 millimetre anti-tank gun – the nemesis of nearly every Allied tank that encountered it.

A woman worker on the Y Block tank build line. The thickness of the frontal armour plate can be seen through the gun port.

above Truck engine assembly line; fitting oil pumps and timing covers.
opposite above Tank engine cylinder block valve seats are checked and given a final polish in Y Block tank shop. A twelve cylinder horizontally opposed side valve petrol engine rated at 350 hp. powered the Churchill tank.
opposite below Checking and grading Bedford truck engine pistons on the assembly line.

Propaganda is an important part of any war effort; in Luton we held a "Warship Week", a "Salute the Soldier" week, and raised money for Spitfires – anything to lift morale and appeal to patriotism.

Monday 22nd September Vauxhall held a "Tanks for Russia" week, when the entire plant, including office boys, was required to work overtime. I doubt that my efforts contributed anything, but I was thrilled and swelled with pride at the sight of our tanks clattering down Kimpton Road covered in painted messages of friendship and support for our gallant allies who were bearing the brunt of the Nazi onslaught.

They were loaded onto ships of the Arctic convoys, and despite losses some eventually reached Murmansk and the embattled Red Army.

Tuesday 30th September A big Army exercise involving thousands of troops is in progress in the countryside around Luton, and the frequent thump of gunfire is heard and felt by night and day.

Wednesday 1st October Ivor and I cycled through Tea Green to Kings Walden this evening; we came upon a battery of field guns manned by Canadian troops in the hollow between Wigmore Hall and Wandon End, their field telephone cables draped all along the roadside hedges.

On K Block assembly line a woman worker uses a heavy torque spanner to fit a truck wheel.

Sunday 5th October I went with Mum and Clarice to hear an excellent concert by the BBC Theatre Orchestra broadcast from the Alma Cinema.

Wednesday 8th October "The Germans are making a huge thrust towards Moscow. Heard "Welcome All" on the radio tonight". Very busy at work – weather sunny and warm.

Wednesday 15th October "Heard the German interrupter on the radio tonight" – a ghostly voice pretending to be a British resistance station and spouting Nazi propaganda.

Chassis assembly operations on the moving track.

Tuesday 21st October "We realise that raids will start in a few weeks".

Wednesday 22nd October "An alert sounded at 9 o'clock and several Jerries went over".

Friday 31st October "The oil burners were going tonight".

Saturday 1st November "Weather dull, cold, hail at times. Finished reading "Fire over England" tonight. Jerry came over and the oil burners were going".

Friday 7th November "Stalin gave a speech last night" – a rallying call to the Soviet people and an appeal for a second front in Europe to relieve the pressure on the Russian forces.

Saturday 8th November "In a terrific raid on Germany last night, we lost 37 bombers".

November 1941 saw the birth of Vauxhall's Management Advisory Committee, an institution that was to be a prominent feature of life at Vauxhall for more than the next thirty years. The first committee was appointed for twelve months and consisted of workers from shop and office floor, Trades Union representatives, foremen and senior managers: initiated by Charles Bartlett, its aim was to deal with any problems causing friction between workers and management before they escalated into disputes and hindered the war effort. By November 1942 electoral constituencies covered the entire plant and the elected M.A.C. took over; its problem solving activities over the years undoubtedly contributing to Vauxhall's reputation for industrial peace in a normally turbulent industry.

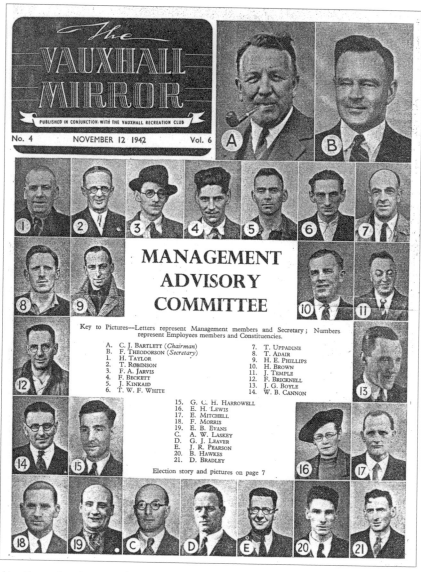

At a time when Joint Production Committees consisting of Trade Unionists and management were being set up all over Britain to help the war effort, Charles Bartlett conceived Vauxhall's own version – the Management Advisory Committee, made up of elected representatives from the Plant's twenty one constituencies, and here featured on the front cover of the Vauxhall Mirror in November 1942.

Tuesday 11th November I managed to buy cigarettes for Dad's birthday tomorrow; they are now in desperately short supply, and at lunchtimes the diners form a long queue at the canteen shop: to ensure fair distribution, the staff have decided to ration everyone to two packets of twenty per week, and stamp the current works' pass/pay envelope with indelible ink to frustrate those who would like a "second helping".

Friday 14th November Sad news. "The grand old Ark Royal was sunk today".

Sunday 23rd November Cycled to Letchworth to spend the day with Russell Rogers and other old friends.

Monday 1st December "Norman Morris came back to work today. The Russians are attacking at Rostov".

Sunday 7th December Cycled to Letchworth today to meet Jack Taylor and call on the Duncombes. Heard on our radio that the Japanese have bombed U.S. Naval bases, so we now have another powerful ally and a further assurance of eventual victory – however long it takes.

Wednesday 10th December "The Prince of Wales and the Repulse have been sunk by the Japs, this is a great blow".

Sunday 14th December "Heavy rain all day so Jack did not visit as arranged; Mum made the Christmas puddings this afternoon".

Monday 15th December As I will be sixteen in a few days, I joined the office fire guard rota. "Ivor's boil burst tonight, heard "The Mistletoe Bough" and "Gaslight" on the radio".

Sunday 21st December Cycled to Hitchin and Kings Walden this morning and gathered holly. Listened to "The Happidrome" tonight; Hitler has taken command of the German army.

Tuesday 23rd December My sixteenth birthday, and as last year Mr Morris "went round with the hat" for the office boys, and I was delighted to discover that my share was sixteen shillings and ninepence – two shillings and three pence more than last year.

Wednesday 24th December Mr Morris handed round a mince pie and a small glass of sherry to each of the staff this afternoon in honour of Christmas; the weather fine and frosty, and a lovely sunset. Heard Churchill broadcast from America tonight and we hung the holly.

Thursday 25th December We had "good things" for dinner and listened to the King's broadcast. In the afternoon, I strolled into town to see Edgar Wallace's "The Return of the Frog" at the Alma Cinema; now sixteen, and a semi secret smoker of cigarettes for over a year and a half, I decided to emulate our manager, Mr Johnson, and purchased a pipe and a one ounce tin of "Three Nuns" curly cut pipe tobacco. Comfortably settled in the stalls, I stuffed in the "Three Nuns", lit my pipe, inhaled deeply and experienced, for some long minutes, a sensation of light-headed euphoria, swiftly followed by a rising tide of nausea which propelled me from my seat, up the aisle, through a door marked "Fire Exit" and into a side alley where I saw dimly in the moonlight, a row of dustbins ranged along the wall. Aware of my urgent need, and not wishing to befoul the alley, I lifted a dustbin lid to find it filled with sour kitchen waste from the Alma's Café, and destined for pig swill; the stench hit my nostrils and my response was quick and violent, as, pallid and sweating, I thankfully donated my Christmas dinner to the pigs. Walking home up Crawley Green Hill under a frosty moon, with pipe and tobacco in my jacket pocket, I decided to keep secret my humiliating attempt at manhood, and spent the rest of the evening sipping soda water and huddled over the fire.

Friday 26th December A fine, frosty Boxing Day, and the Vauxhall plant returned to work. Enjoyed "The Kentucky Minstrels" tonight and we listened to yet another Churchill speech from America.

Vauxhall's plant and its workforce had undergone a transformation in the previous twelve months; we had been visited and inspected by Winston Churchill, King George, the Duke of Kent and a dozen other VIPs; new facilities had been built, new models like the QL 4 x 4 truck were introduced, and our tank production was gaining momentum, and all our products, from trucks to tanks, were constantly modified, refined and improved. The greatest change, however, was in the workforce, as Ernest Bevin's Ministry of Labour directed thousands of women to replace men on machining lines and assembly tracks; smoking was now permitted in most areas with hundreds of red painted ashtrays fixed to stanchions and walls, whilst "Music whilst you work" battled with the din of the workshops to relieve the tedium of day or nightshift hours spent on repetitive work. The resilience of Luton's people had triumphed over the misery and despondency of January, and had slowly, month by month, evolved into a quiet confidence. As always, New Year's Eve was a time for reflection on the past year and apprehension for the future; the Alliance of Britain, the Soviet Union and the United States had drastically shifted the balance of power in our favour compared with seven months ago, when, alone, we faced the Nazi monster; as my diary noted in its final comment in the last hours of 1941; "so ends a year in which Hitler's doom was sealed".

Epilogue

Everyone sensed that 1942 was a turning point in the war, although none imagined that peace was still three and a half years in the future; the threat of a concentrated Nazi attack still hung over Luton and Vauxhall, and for the next three years we cursed and gasped for breath in the smoke on moonlit nights, our sleep still disturbed by the sirens and the occasional thump of bombs nearby, and on a brilliant Saturday morning in September, with no warning from the town's sirens, a single bomb whistled down, missed Midland Road Railway station by two hundred yards and killed five people.

A convoy of MW 15cwt and OY 3 ton trucks assembled in Kimpton Road on a bleak Winter's day before a mass drive away to army transport depots.

A group of Y Block workers pose proudly in front of a finished tank; this was a later 40 ton model with a larger turret and a 75mm gun.

Our new allies soon made their presence felt, when the vanguard of the many thousands of smartly-uniformed, well-paid American troops were seen on Luton's streets, and in October a group of Red Army officers visiting Vauxhall received an ecstatic welcome in the works' canteen; a show of appreciation for the heroic Russian stand at Stalingrad.

The Spring of 1942 was also a turning point in my career at Vauxhall when I gained an apprenticeship, completed my two year stint of servitude, said my farewells to Mr Morris and Arthur Fulcher, introduced my successor, John Brown, to the complexities of our filing system and handed over the keys to the Planning Department's bike.

Monday 4th May I donned my new boiler suit and joined the lads of the Trade School in P Block, along with the rest of the Spring intake, to learn the essentials of engineering: our instructors, a patient, dedicated staff of fine craftsmen who taught us cocky, often fractious boys, the arts

Norman
seeks
tank
team

RECOGNISE yourself in this group picture, sent to the *Mirror* by Norman Morris? He believes it was taken during the war when he was involved in tank work.
Norman, supervisor of the planning and tool department, is in the second row, fourth from the left. Also in the picture, he recalls, Walter Hill (front row, fifth from left) and in the second row (on the far left) is Bob Wilkinson, then manager, production control.
Norman, now 89 and living in Leagrave, Luton, wonders whether any other member of this war-time group would like to contact him.
"I can't get about much these days but I would love to hear from any of them," said Norman, who retired in 1962 after just over 43 years' service.
If any member of this group would like to get in touch with Norman, the *Mirror* will be glad to pass on his address.

Association news round up   by Peter Vigor

AUTUMN HOLIDAY
SPECIAL!

Autumn Holiday at
Sand Bay
Weston-super-Mare

This is the team of production engineers and planners responsible for the tooling and production of the Churchill tank during the second World War, and includes my boss, Norman Morris, who was in charge of the records office; the group are posed at the rear of the canteen where a glimpse of the distant roof of X Block can be seen in the background. Norman sent this picture to the "Vauxhall Mirror" in 1986 when he was 89 years of age. Those whose names I remember are:

Left to right: Front row: 3. Monty Johnson Chief production engineer.
6. Reg. Pearson Plant Manager. 8. Arthur Thursby Asst. production engineer.
9.H. P. Mott Planner. 10. Bob Buckle Machine maintenance.
Centre row: 1. Bob Wilkinson Production control. 4. Norman Morris Planning records.
6. Tom Reynolds Planner. 7. John Arnold Planner. 8. Ted Pennington Planner. 10. Bill Barker Machine maintenance. 11. Arthur Potter Planner gear boxes.
Back Row. 4. Rick Norris Tool stores. 5. John Helliwell Tool room. 7. Ben Holloway Tool design. 8. Frank Lane Planner. 10. Walter Rigby Chief Tool inspector. 11. Horace Dennet Tool contact.

of bench fitting, turning, milling, grinding and welding, and who are today fondly remembered: Arthur Chappel, George Ingledew, Harry Ealing, "Foo" Newbury, Gus Eaton and Harry Garrett; and our chief instructor Harold "Budgie" Elson – so nicknamed because of his misshapen nose, who, as a sixteen year old apprentice in 1909, had been one of the Vauxhall engineering team that built the Brooklands record breaking KN race car: whilst the first floor housed the classrooms where Jock Beattie and "Binky" Brash struggled to implant the theoretical aspects of engineering in wayward minds, normally pre-occupied with girls, beer, music and films.

Our workshops were directly involved in the war effort, turning out hundreds of tank engine assembly tools, case openers, and even gun sights for Vauxhall's Home Guard. Third year apprentices were assigned to various departments (or divisions in Vauxhall parlance) where they would probably make their future career; in my case, I was directed to Quality Control – or Inspection as it was then known – and for the next two years I worked under the supervision of Wilf Colbourne in the gear shop, Bill Chown in back axles and bevel gears in P Block, and Fred Parsons on the engine test beds and dynamometers.

In September 1942, Vauxhall's new factory in Boscombe Road, Dunstable, began to produce tank engines to supplement Luton's production, and to overhaul and repair engines returned from active service with army units. Also in the Autumn of 1942 the Luton factory was visited by the distinguished War Artist, Eric Kennington, seeking subjects for his book, "Tanks and Tank Folk", a celebration of the workers who built them and the soldiers who manned them in battle; in Y Block he met Tom Adair – a Glaswegian working on the tank engine cylinder block line – and decided to portray him as he operated his radial drill. Tom's search for work had led him, like many of his fellow

right Eric Kennington, a distinguished sculptor and official war artist in both World Wars, visited the Vauxhall Plant in 1942, seeking subjects for his book about tanks and the workers who built them; in Y Block he met Tom Adair, a union shop steward and a newly-elected member of the Management Advisory Committee whom he portrayed at his work station on the tank engine cylinder block line. The portrait hung in the Director's Board Room for 25 years and was presented to Tom on his retirement in 1967.

countrymen, to Luton in 1938, and in 1940 he joined Vauxhall, working as a machinist in the newly-built Y Block, and by 1941 he was elected Engineering Union Shop Steward for the Tank shop and was appointed to the first Management Advisory Committee.

Kennington's portrait of Tom hung in the Directors' Board Room for more than 25 years, and when he retired in 1967 it was presented to him; a memento of his own working life, and also of the time when Luton's car makers became armament manufacturers. He died in 1986, and, when I interviewed his widow Isobel, she told me she had given the portrait to her grandson, Kenneth Adair, as Kennington had all too faithfully painted the hole in Tom's jumper, and it was a constant reminder to her that she never got round to mending it.

On a dull, dank Sunday morning of the 15th November, all the church bells of Luton and the surrounding villages rang out – after a silence of almost three years – to celebrate the victory at Alamein and uplift our hearts.

Mother's health steadily declined, with increasingly frequent spells in hospital and confinement to bed at home, and reached a low point just at the time when the Nazis' "buzz bombs" or "doodle bugs" began to arrive in Luton in June 1944; during at least six alerts, they passed overhead with the rasping sound of an un-silenced motor cycle engine and two exploded – one on open land at Lewsey farm and the other which damaged houses in Stopsley.

Monday 31st July "Mum was taken to St Mary's hospital this afternoon. Dr Eberlie says she will die any day".

Tuesday 1st August I left the gear shop at 9 a.m. and arrived at the hospital a few minutes after Mum died. I was not allowed to see her and I had to wait until the afternoon when Dad, Clarice, Ivor and I saw her for the last time in the little mortuary by the hospital's Dallow Road entrance gate. Three days later she was laid to rest with her father in

Once Churchill tanks were made in Gipsy Lane. Luton's Parkway Rail station and the Retail Park now occupy the site of Vauxhall's Y Block tank shop.

Letchworth cemetery, mourned by all her old friends and neighbours. "Doodle bugs" continued to pass overhead until mid November, but Luton still had to suffer one more terrible attack from the air.

Monday 6th November Luton's other truck manufacturer, Commer Karrier Ltd, was hit by a V2 rocket which devastated Biscot Road, killed nineteen people and injured almost two hundred – the thunderous explosion and huge mushroom cloud still remembered with horror by many old Lutonians.

Victory came in that glorious May of 1945, when the nation emerged battered, bankrupt, and delirious with joy: when it required a great effort of memory to recall the desperation and seemingly hopeless future that faced us a mere five years before. When the celebrations subsided,

The 200,000th wartime Bedford, a QL 4x4 General Service truck driven by an ATS Corporal leads a column of army trucks through the P Block vehicle delivery gate to commence its duty with the Army.

there was time to take stock and reflect on the trials and tribulations of the past six years and assess Vauxhall's contribution to victory.

Charles Bartlett was knighted in the 1944 New Year's Honours List for his services to Britain's war effort: and by the end of the war almost a quarter of a million trucks had rolled off Vauxhall's assembly lines and 5,640 Churchill tanks were built. Credit for the tanks must be shared with the foundries, forges, steel mills and arsenals who supplied the turret castings, hulls and weapons, and also the ten "shadow factories", many with experience of heavy engineering, such as Newton Chambers and Harland and Wolfe; nevertheless, the project was conceived and directed by Vauxhall; all the engineering, design, development and testing was done at Luton, and all the engines produced there.

It has to be conceded that our tank was never a match for the enemy's in terms of hitting power, speed, or defensive armour, but, despite this, it acquitted itself well in North Africa, Italy, Normandy and Germany in its "Crocodile flame thrower" and "Flying Dustbin" versions, in assaulting fortified bunkers; but above all, it filled a vital gap when the British army had virtually no heavy armour and the need was desperately urgent.

In considering the story of Luton's Blitzkrieg, one nagging question recurs – one enduring mystery remains – why was Luton never specifically targeted by the Luftwaffe? A sizeable industrial town, producing large quantities of motor transport, heavy tanks, ball bearings, shells, Mosquito bombers and a host of other munitions, ranging from mortars to marine equipment and uniforms; a tempting target one would think for Goering's bombers.

The town was within easy reach of the bomber bases on the Continent, and the enemy's carefully annotated aerial reconnaissance photographs captured at the War's end, show that they had accurate knowledge of Luton and its industries.

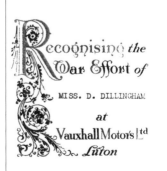

THE Management and Workers of Vauxhall Motors Ltd., Luton, acknowledge and appreciate the tremendous part played by those who joined the Company during the war years, 1939 onwards, to take the place of men in the Forces and to assist in the manufacture of nearly a quarter of a million trucks, and the development and production of the Churchill Tank. They thank you—and they will not forget.

A thank you from "the Skipper", Managing Director, Sir Charles Bartlett, to Dorothy Dillingham – just one of the thousands of women who made such a vital contribution to Vauxhall's wartime production of trucks and tanks.

The Luftwaffe had given a chilling demonstration of its ability to pinpoint and destroy a target with the attack on Coventry at a time when the RAF was experiencing great difficulty in locating its targets in Germany and an error of 5 miles was considered accurate.

Yet most of the raids appeared to be random, or attacks on "targets of opportunity" – even the raid of the 30th August would seem to fall into this category, when the raiding force was driven off its intended target – the East Anglian fighter stations – and released its bomb load over the airport and Vauxhall. The authorities almost certainly expected a saturation raid and took elaborate measures to hide the town, the Vauxhall plant, the airport and the Skefco factories in particular; whilst most Luton citizens also feared that our town might suffer Coventry's fate – but, for whatever reason, the threat failed to materialize – a fact for which we are all eternally thankful.

The war memorial in Kimpton Road lists Vauxhall's war dead: the bronze plaques were originally sited at the top of the steps into the main canteen, but when it was demolished in the nineteen nineties, the present memorial was erected where P Block once stood.

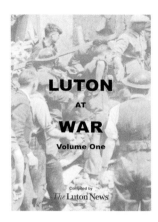 

LUTON AT WAR
Volume One & Volume Two

Initially published by the Luton News in 1947, the story of how the people of Luton withstood the dark years of war between 1939 and 1945. Luton and its population have changed so dramatically in the years since the war that now only a few will recall how the town stood up to the trauma of those war years.

Because of strict war-time censorship much of what occurred during those years was not mentioned in The Luton News. Once the war was over however, The Luton News set about the mammoth task of presenting a complete and vivid picture of war-time life. It tells of the long anxious nights, the joy and the sorrow that made even the most terrifying moments bearable thanks to the tremendous way in which the people joined to help each other.

Written and compiled by the staff of The Luton News at the time, it contains the most comprehensive and fascinating pictorial record. As well as being a moving personal account it is also a unique historical document.

Published in a large format paperback in two parts.

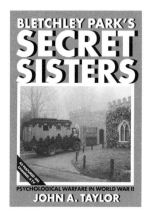

BLETCHLEY PARK'S SECRET SISTERS
Psychological Warfare in World War II

John A. Taylor

Bletchley Park will be forever associated with the secret intelligence activities of World War Two. Yet in addition to the incredible achievements of the code breakers, only a few miles away several other secret organisations were also achieving clandestine success, with operations that were conducted from centres scattered around the local area. This region had been chosen by the Government because it was remote from the London Blitz yet still maintained good road and rail communications with the Capital – but what did these secret organisations do?

In a highly subversive campaign, propaganda played an early and effective role, selecting recruits from amongst the refugees fleeing Nazi oppression. Gathered in large, local houses, there they would write and rehearse propaganda scripts for radio broadcasts to enemy territory. At a secret studio, these broadcasts were then recorded onto discs and taken by the Secret Service to radio transmitting stations hidden in the local countryside.

Under the control of the Communications Section of the Secret Intelligence Service, another radio station transmitted decoded information from Bletchley Park to Allied military commanders overseas. Further radio stations maintained contact with secret agents, sent on missions deep inside Occupied Europe. In hidden workshops, advanced radio equipment for their use was designed and manufactured, and in various country houses specialised training schools were set up.

Later in the war, not far from Woburn Abbey an ultra modern recording and broadcast studio was built which, when linked to the most powerful radio transmitter in Europe, began sophisticated operations that would completely deceive the Germans. In just one example, actual German radio stations were taken over and, by mimicking the original announcers, all manner of false instructions could then be put out to confuse the German listeners.

This book tells the little known story of all these other secret activities, the fascinating story of Bletchley Park's 'Secret Sisters'.

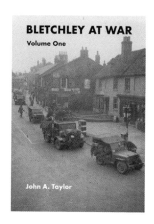

BLETCHLEY AT WAR
Volume One

John A. Taylor

BLETCHLEY AT WAR
Volume 1

John A. Taylor

The wartime story of Bletchley Park is now world famous, the achievements of the codebreakers, their influence on world events, and the introduction of electronic computers that laid the foundations of the modern world.

Thousands of personnel were employed at Bletchley Park throughout the Second World War – 'the geese that laid the golden eggs and never cackled' – in the oft quoted words of Winston Churchill. Throughout the Second World war many were billetted in the town, yet little has been told about the everyday life of Bletchley during this period. The rationing, the blackout, the Home Guard, firewatching, incessant army convoys, loved ones serving abroad, air raid alerts, and so much more, that was different from the peacetime years.

It was a time of trauma and change, not only for the adults, but also for the children, and not least the hundreds of evacuees who, separated from their parents and their familiar surroundings, came to seek refuge with new families, sometimes with laughter and sometimes with tears. A world very different from today, and in a chapter especially for the younger generation, with her young friends, Naomi Wellard explores a way of life unknown to children of today. A time not of designer clothes, computers and mobile phones, but of gas masks, guns and going without.

Bletchley at War reveals how the ordinary people coped at an extraordinary time, and introduces the reader to the everyday matters and the everyday people, the shopkeepers, the officials, and the many personalities who helped maintain morale in a time of unending uncertainty.

In thoroughly researched detail, with many rare photographs, and extending to three volumes, here is the story of Bletchley at War, the wartime Bletchley of Bletchley Park.

Pip Brimson

BUCKINGHAM AT WAR

Pip Brimson

The people of Buckingham adapted well to a state of war. Their stories reflect courage, humour and occasional pathos.

How they coped with A.R.P., gas masks, blackout, mobilization and the secrets of Bletchley Park, followed by the formation of the Home Guard, Land Girls, and the jobs women were directed to. The progress of the war through those early years, which included rationing and evacuation, individual efforts by those at home and fund raising events in the town are all related in this book. The collection of salvage took a large part – as did the knitting of comforts for the Forces by local women's groups. Everything was geared for eventual Victory, however long it might take.

When at last the end of the War approached, the blackout was lifted; the Home Guard, their job finished, stood down, and prisoners of war overseas began to return home to great rejoicing, which culminated on V.E. and V.J. Days. Servicemen too, were slowly beginning to demobilize.

Finally, everyone could sit back and take stock – attend to their losses and sadness, but feel proud of what had been achieved – and then, begin to prepare for the problems and happiness Peace would bring, after long years of struggle and endeavour.

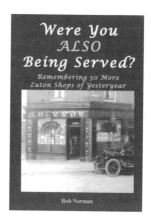

WERE YOU BEING SERVED?
and
WERE YOU *ALSO* BEING SERVED?

Bob Norman

In this present era of organised but monotonous chain-stores, Bob Norman has recalled the days of the independently owned shops and services where personal attention was foremost. Through reminiscence with family descendents and past employees, thanks to these books they will not be forgotten. The two volumes together contain one hundred Luton storylines with historical facts and anecdotes chronicled in an interesting and entertaining style.

From the preface by John Buckledee, Editor, The Luton News
"I have a fair idea of the amount of dedicated work such books involve. The Luton News publishes every week a feature called Yesteryear which includes an old photograph and appropriate details. It's enormously popular but it takes a prodigious amount of time and effort to produce, and woe betide The Luton News if a single detail is incorrect! So I have great admiration for his achievement in discovering so many fascinating and unpublished stories.

In these pages are a goldmine of shopping stories and information. I predict another best-seller."

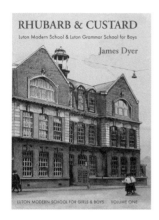

RHUBARB & CUSTARD
Luton Modern School & Luton Grammar School for Boys

James Dyer

LUTON MODERN SCHOOL FOR GIRLS & BOYS   VOLUME ONE

LUTON MODERN SCHOOL FOR GIRLS & BOYS

Volume 1 RHUBARB AND CUSTARD
Luton Modern School &
Luton Grammar School for Boys
James Dyer
.
Volume 2 CRIMSON AND GOLD
Luton Modern School, Luton High School
for Girls and Luton Technical School
Anne Allsopp

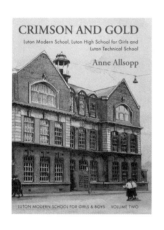

CRIMSON AND GOLD
Luton Modern School, Luton High School for Girls and
Luton Technical School

Anne Allsopp

LUTON MODERN SCHOOL FOR GIRLS & BOYS   VOLUME TWO

Luton Secondary Day School began life amongst the noise of trams, the bustle of market stalls and the pungent smell of hops from the neighbouring brewery, in a disused hat factory off Park Square in September 1904. Four years later the newly built Luton Modern School opened on the east side of Park Square, close to the Parish Church. It admitted 170 mainly fee-paying boys and girls, with room for at least a hundred more, under the firm rule of Thomas Sanderson. After the Great War, in which 38 old boys died, the number of applications for admission necessitated the girls moving to a new site in temporary wooden huts in Alexandra Avenue. Under the Headship of the formidable Helen K. Sheldon the school went from strength to strength, acquiring a fine new building in 1930. The boys educational requirements rapidly outgrew the Modern School premises, with its inconvenient sports facilities at Chaul End. In 1938 they moved into an award-winning building with 23 acres of playing fields at Bradgers Hill. During the Headship of Kenneth B. Webb, in 1944, it changed its name to Luton Grammar School. From 1937 the Junior Technical School, under Dr Sidney Charlesworth, took over the Park Square buildings, affectionately known as 'The Tech', and rapidly outgrew them, but having to wait until 1958 before they could move to a purpose built school with ample playing fields at Barnfield Avenue. These books finish when the three Schools were dissolved in the late 1960s, to be replaced by the Luton Sixth Form College.

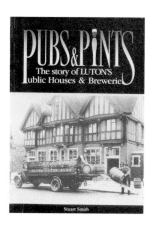

PUBS & PINTS
The story of Luton's Public Houses and Breweries

Stuart Smith

Whilst the town of Luton is well documented in other ways, this book is the first comprehensive history of its important brewing industry and retail beer outlets – linked, staple trades in the area for over five hundred years.

The development of the modern public house from the early taverns and coaching inns closely followed that of the breweries, with the final decades of the last century seen as the high point in the number of houses licensed to sell beers for consumption on or off the premises. Since then the total has declined with the loss of around 40% during the last one hundred years, most of these losses occurring in the period from 1950 to 1970.

Although documentation dealing with the early breweries and public houses is extremely sparse, it is the intention of this book to try and record the history of each brewery and public house that has had its bearing on the social and drinking pastimes of Lutonians over the last one hundred and fifty years. A special feature of this book is the vast range of three hundred photographs – many old, rare and unusual.

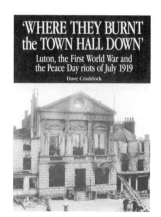

"WHERE THEY BURNT THE TOWN HALL DOWN"
Luton, The First World War and the Peace day Riots of July 1919

Dave Craddock

The weekend of 19/20th July 1919 was arguably the most momentous in the history of Luton. What began as an afternoon of peace celebrations marking the end of the Great War turned into riots that had by the Sunday morning left the Town hall a smouldering, gutted ruin with the military in control of the town. Yet over the years, the story of the riots has been largely neglected.

Drawing broadly on contemporary documents, witness statements and newspaper reports, the book gives a blow-by-blow account of the riots, their aftermath and subsequent trials. The hostility between the Town Council and ex-servicemen's organisations in the preceding months is also covered extensively, as is the impact of the First World War on Luton.

Features of this book include informative appendices containing a wealth of information and over 50 illustrations.

THE CHANGING FACE OF LUTON

Stephen Bunker, Robin Holgate & Marian Nichols

The Changing Face of Luton traces the fortunes of the settlement and economy of the town from the earliest recorded arrival of people in the area to the present day. It looks at different aspects of Luton and its development rather than giving a straight chronological account of its history.

Luton's roots go back a very long way, yet in less than 200 years it has changed from a small market town to today's busy industrial and commercial centre. This transformation is described, helped by a range of excellent photographs, thereby answering many of the questions frequently asked, and perhaps raising more, about this intriguing town.

The three authors from Luton Museum are all experts in local history, archaeology and industry.

THE STOPSLEY BOOK
and
THE STOPSLEY PICTURE BOOK

James Dyer

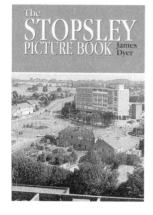

The hamlet of Stopsley, two miles from Luton in Bedfordshire, has a history that stretches back some 300,000 years. Situated in a region initially dependent on agriculture, straw plaiting and brick making, it can be seen as a microcosm of life in almost any village on the northern edge of the Chiltern Hills.

The Stopsley Book tells the story of 20 farms, 16 schools and 4 churches within the civil parish which stretched from Someries Castle in the south to Galley Hill and the Icknield Way in the north. It looks in detail at almost every aspect of village life, particularly in the 19th and 20th centuries, and includes the work of the Parish Council, the weather, water and gas supplies, health care, policing, farm work, brick making and a wide variety of leisure pursuits. Based on thirty years of extensive search and interviews with local people, many now deceased, it is an exhaustive account of a community that still prides itself on its village spirit and individuality.

It includes a collection of 146 photographs, many of which have not been published before. A revised edition was published in 2005.

The Stopsley Book aroused such a great deal of interest in Britain and abroad that a number of readers submitted archive photographs of Stopsley and its surrounding area to the author. These are included in *The Stopsley Picture Book*, which contains 150 photographs and carefully researched captions, to supplement the original work.

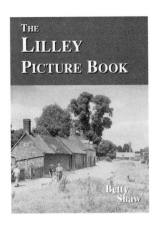

THE LILLEY PICTURE BOOK

Betty Shaw

For some years pictures of the old village of Lilley in Hertfordshire have formed a popular feature at the Flower Festivals held each May in St.Peter's Church. Though some photos date back to the late nineteenth century, this book mainly focuses on activities in the village during the twentieth century. During that time the Church, and the Sowerby family as Lords of the manor, largely dominated village life and most of the populace were engaged in agriculture-related activities. By the latter half of the century, with little new housing development and rising property prices, many of the younger people moved away, leading indirectly to the closure of the village school and numerous small shops. New financially enhanced families moved into some of the cottages, renovating and improving them. In the closing years of the century the Sowerby family sold the Manor and left Lilley. Today, whilst many of the children are bussed to nearby schools, the adult population make their living by commuting to neighbouring towns or travelling to London and the wider world beyond. Farming, once the mainstay of the village life, is now highly mechanised and depends largely on occasional contract labour. At the beginning of the new century, whilst to the eyes of visitors it remains an attractive rural haven, frequented by ramblers and sightseers, it is still a living village with a church, two popular public houses and many activities in its recently modernised village hall.

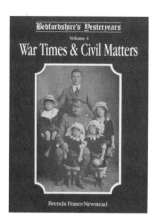

BEDFORDSHIRE'S YESTERYEARS
Volume 4
War Times & Civil Matters

Brenda Fraser-Newstead

Social history comes to life, first-hand and vivid, when seen through the eyes of those who experienced and shaped it.

The 'Bedfordshire's Yesteryears' series contains many privileged glimpses of a way of life that has changed radically. Here is the generation of two World Wars; here are the witnesses to countless technological and sociological transformations.

This volume highlights the angst of the Depression and the two World Wars, when the whole social fabric was disrupted but showed extraordinary resilience. It also traces another major feature of the twentieth century, namely the rapid development in all modes of transport – carriers and trams, airships and fire-engines, trains and automobiles.

Route marches, the General Strike, the Home Guard, the munitions factory, the Land Army, barrage balloons, evacuees, G.I. brides, the Specials, steam fire-engines, double-decker trams, the concert party – just a few of the evocative words that roll away the decades.

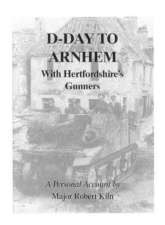

D-DAY TO ARNHEM
With Hertfordshire's Gunners

Major Robert Kiln

There are many books about D-Day and the subsequent defeat of the German Army in Normandy between June and August 1944, but not many have been written by those who took part in the fighting on the ground. This account, drawn from the diaries and memories of the author and others in the HertfordshireYeomanry 86th Field Regiment RA, provides a vivid picture of their basic training, preparations for D-Day, the landing itself, the fierce battles in the Normandy bocage country until the August breakthrough, and the rapid advance to Antwerp, where the author was wounded and evacuated in early September. A brief postscript carries the regiment on to its disbandment in April 1946.

The text is complemented by 48 photographs and 26 maps detailing all the movements described by the author.

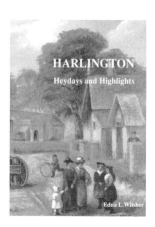

HARLINGTON HEYDAYS AND HIGHLIGHTS

Edna L.Wilsher

A journey on a golden September afternoon in 1996 from her home in Silsoe to Harlington, Bedfordshire, the village of her birth, awakened the author's memories to past events in her life. Harlington's connections with the evangelist, John Bunyan are featured, linking with her own early childhood when she attended the village school by the church.

The quiet little village came alive with the arrival of evacuees from London at the beginning of the war, thereafter never to be the same again. Her own journalistic career at Home Counties Newspapers was put on hold when she was called into the Auxiliary Territorial Service, stationed in London with V1 and V2 bombs falling all around, and nostalgic thoughts of Harlington crossed her mind, although it, too, had its own wartime traumas.

Historical pageantry came with the opening of the new village hall, returning again for its fiftieth anniversary celebrations. The millennium is also highlighted.

After marriage, the author became a freelance writer for national magazines. Her inspiration for this story was drawn from a very special award-winning painting, featured on the cover of this book.

A HATFUL OF MUSIC
The Dance Band Days in Luton, Dunstable & District

Stuart Goodyear

In 1939 Lutonian Stuart Goodyear was born into a musical household, whose father, also Stuart, encouraged him to embrace his love of music.

As a millennium project, Stuart was asked by the Luton Historical Society to write a page or two about the local "dance band days" of the last century, and drawing on his own involvement as novice pianist through to bandleader, was happy to undertake the challenge.

Starting in a modest way in the 1950s with fellow airport apprentices, his first band The Rainbow Melody Makers, rapidly became a larger and more polished dance band, and was subsequently renamed The Ray Miller Band. Remaining as leader of the band through to the 1980s, he became well connected with the local musical establishment, and has comprehensively collated his experiences during that time, although it soon became apparent that the finished article would be a book, rather than a dossier.

In a most fascinating personal and wider-ranging survey of musical days gone by in Luton, Dunstable and the surrounding area, Stuart has compiled a detailed impression of how he remembered the busy dance scene, and the many brilliant musicians who contributed to a period of live musical entertainment that will never return.

Deliberating over a title, he shortlisted "Batons and Bows" and "You've gotta lot to learn my boy", but thinks that a "Hatful of Music" just about strikes the right chord. The book contains over 300 photos of events covered over the years. People born and bred in Luton will be pouring over the nostalgia for weeks to come.

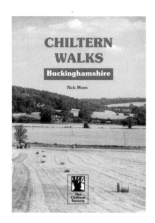
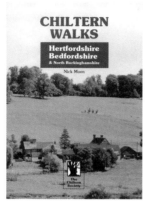
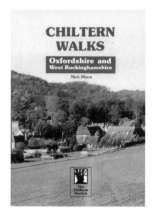

CHILTERN WALKS
Hertfordshire, Bedfordshire and North Buckinghamshire

CHILTERN WALKS
Buckinghamshire

CHILTERN WALKS
Oxfordshire and West Buckinghamshire

Nick Moon

A series of three books to providing a comprehensive coverage of walks throughout the whole of the Chiltern area (as defined by the Chiltern Society). The walks included vary in length from 3.0 to 10.9 miles, but are mainly in the 5–7 mile range popular for half-day walks, although suggestions of possible combinations of walks are given for those preferring a full day's walk.

Each walk gives details of nearby places of interest and is accompanied by a specially drawn map of the route which also indicates local pubs and a skeleton road network.